THE
FUGITIVE SLAVE LAW
AND
ITS VICTIMS

THE
FUGITIVE SLAVE LAW
AND
ITS VICTIMS

Revised and Enlarged Edition

By
SAMUEL MAY

The Black Heritage Library Collection

 BOOKS FOR LIBRARIES PRESS
FREEPORT, NEW YORK
1970

First Published 1861
Reprinted 1970

Reprinted from a copy in the
Fisk University Library Negro Collection

INTERNATIONAL STANDARD BOOK NUMBER:
0-8369-8716-0

LIBRARY OF CONGRESS CATALOG CARD NUMBER:
77-133161

PRINTED IN THE UNITED STATES OF AMERICA

ANTI-SLAVERY TRACTS. No. 15. New Series.

THE

FUGITIVE SLAVE LAW

AND

ITS VICTIMS.

REVISED AND ENLARGED EDITION.

" Thou shalt not deliver unto his master the servant which is escaped from his master unto thee : He shall dwell with thee, even among you, in that place which he shall choose in one of thy gates, where it liketh him best : THOU SHALT NOT OPPRESS HIM." — DEUT. 23 : 15, 16.

NEW YORK:

PUBLISHED BY THE AMERICAN ANTI-SLAVERY SOCIETY.

1861.

☞ In a record like the present, dealing so largely with facts and dates, perfect accuracy is hardly to be expected, although great pains have been taken to make it strictly correct. Any information, on good authority, which will help to make the record more exact, or more complete, will be gratefully received. It should be addressed to SAMUEL MAY, JR., 221 Washington Street, Boston.

THE FUGITIVE SLAVE LAW AND ITS VICTIMS.

THE Fugitive Slave Law was enacted by Congress in September, 1850, received the signature of HOWELL COBB, [of Georgia,] as Speaker of the House of Representatives, of WILLIAM R. KING, [of Alabama,] as President of the Senate, and was "approved," September 18th, of that year, by MILLARD FILLMORE, [of New York,] Acting President of the United States.

The authorship of the Bill is generally ascribed to JAMES M. MASON, Senator from Virginia. Before proceeding to the principal object of this tract, it is proper to give a sy nopsis of the Act itself, which was well called, by the New York *Evening Post*, "An Act for the Encouragement of Kidnapping." It is in ten sections.

SYNOPSIS OF THE LAW.

SECTION 1. United States Commissioners "authorized and required to exercise and discharge all the powers and duties conferred by this act."

SECT. 2. Commissioners for the Territories to be appointed by the Superior Court of the same.

SECT. 3. United States Circuit Courts, and Superior Courts of Territories, required to enlarge the number of Commissioners, "with a view to afford reasonable facilities to reclaim fugitives from labor," &c.

SECT. 4. Commissioners put on the same footing with Judge s o f the United States Courts, with regard to enforcing the Law and its penalties.

SECT. 5. United States Marshals and Deputy Marshals, who may refuse to act under the Law, to be fined one thousand dollars, to the use of the claimant. If a fugitive escape from the custody of a Marshal, the Marshal to be liable for his full value. Commissioners authorized to appoint special officers, and to call out the *posse comitatus*, &c.

SECT. 6. The claimant of any fugitive slave, or his attorney, "may pursue and reclaim such fugitive person," either by procuring a warrant from some Judge or Commissioner, " or by seizing and arresting such fugitive, where the same can be done without process ; " to take such fugitive before such Judge or Commissioner, " whose duty it shall be to hear and determine the case of such claimant in a summary manner," and, if satisfied of the identity of the prisoner, to grant a certificate to said `aimant to "remove such fugitive person back to the State or Territory from whence he or she may have escaped,"—using "such reasonable force or restraint as may be necessary under the circumstances of the case." " In no trial or hearing under this act shall the testimony of such alleged fugitive be admitted in evidence." All molestation of the claimant, in the removal of his slave, "by any process issued by any court, judge, magistrate, or other person whomsoever," prohibited.

SECT. 7. Any person obstructing the arrest of a fugitive, or attempting his or her rescue, or aiding him or her to escape, or harboring and concealing a fugitive, knowing him to be such, shall be subject to a fine of not exceeding one thousand dollars, and to be imprisoned not exceeding six months, and shall also "forfeit and pay the sum of one thousand dollars for each fugitive so *lost*."

SECT. 8. Marshals, deputies, clerks and special officers to receive usual fees ; Commissioners to receive ten dollars, if fugitive is given up to claimant ; otherwise, five dollars ; to be paid by claimant.

SECT. 9. If claimant make affidavit that he fears a rescue of such fugitive from his possession, the officer making the arrest to retain him in custody, and " to remove him to the State whence he fled." Said officer " to employ so many persons as he may deem necessary." All, while so employed, to be paid out of the Treasury of the United States."

SECT. 10. [This section provides an additional and wholly distinct method for the capture of a fugitive ; and, it may be added, one of the loosest and most extraordinary that ever appeared on the pages of a statute book.] Any person, from whom one held to service or labor has escaped, upon making " satisfactory proof" of such escape before any court of record, or judge thereof in vacation, — a record of matters so proved shall be made by such court, or judge, and also a description of the person escaping, "with such convenient certainty as may be ; " — a copy of which record, duly attested, "being produced in any other State, Territory or District," and "being exhibited to any Judge, Commissioner, or other officer authorized," — shall be held and taken to be full and conclusive evidence of the fact of escape, and that the service or labor of the person escaping is due to the party in such record mentioned ; " when, on satisfactory proof of identity, " he or she shall be delivered up to the claimant." " *Provided*, That nothing herein contained shall be construed as requiring the production of a transcript of such record as evidence as aforesaid ; but in its absence, the claim shall be heard and determined upon other satisfactory proofs competent in law."

The names of the NORTHERN men who voted for this infamous kidnapping law should not be forgotten. Until they repent, and do works meet for repentance, their names will stand high and conspicuous on the roll of infamy. Let the " slow-moving finger of scorn " point them out, when they walk among men, and the stings of shame, disappointment and remorse continually visit them in secret, till they are forced to cry, "my punishment is greater than I can bear." As to the *Southern* men who voted for the Law, they only appeared in their legitimate character of oppressors of the poor—whom God will repay, in his own time. The thousand-tongued voices of their brother's blood cry against them from the ground.

The following is the vote, in the SENATE, on the engrossment of the bill : —

YEAS. — Atchison, Badger, Barnwell, Bell, Berrien, Butler, Davis (of Mississippi), Dawson, A. C. DODGE (of Iowa), Downs, Foote, Houston, Hunter, JONES (of Iowa), King, Mangum, Mason, Pearce, Rusk, Sebastian, Soulé, Spruance, STURGEON (of Pennsylvania), Turney, Underwood, Wales, Yulee — 27.

NAYS. — Baldwin, Bradbury, Chase, Cooper, Davis (of Massachusetts), Dayton, Henry Dodge (of Wisconsin), Greene, Smith, Upham, Walker, Winthrop — 12.

ABSENT, OR NOT VOTING. — Benton, Borland, *Bright* of Indiana, *Clarke* of Rhode Island, Clay, *Cass* of Michigan, Clemens, *Dickinson* of New York, *Douglas* of Illinois, *Ewing* of Ohio, *Felch* of Michigan, *Hale* of New Hampshire, *Hamlin* of Maine, *Miller* of New Jersey, *Morton*, *Norris* of New Hampshire, *Phelps* of Vermont, Pratt, *Seward* of New York, *Shields* of Illinois, *Whitcomb* of Indiana. [Fifteen Northern Senators absent from the vote.]

On the final passage of the bill in the Senate, the yeas and nays were not taken. *D. S. Dickinson*, of New York, who had been absent when the vote was taken on the engrossment, spoke in favor of the bill. Mr. Seward was said to be absent from the city, detained by ill health.

When the Bill came up in the HOUSE OF REPRESENTATIVES, (September 12th,) JAMES THOMPSON, of Pennsylvania, got the floor,—probably by a previous understanding with the Speaker, — and addressed the House in support of the Bill. He closed his remarks by *moving the previous question!* It was ordered, and thus all opportunity for reply, and for discussion of the Bill, was cut off. The Bill was then passed to its third reading — equivalent to enactment — by a vote of 109 YEAS to 75 Nays; as follows : —

YEAS.

Maine. — THOMAS J. D. FULLER, of Calais ; ELBRIDGE GERRY, of Waterford ; NATHANIEL S. LITTLEFIELD, of Bridgton.

New Hampshire. — HARRY HIBBARD, of Bath ; CHARLES H. PEASLEE, of Concord.

Massachusetts. — SAMUEL A. ELIOT, of Boston.

New York. — HIRAM WALDEN, of Waldensville.

New Jersey. — ISAAC WILDRICK, of Blairstown.

Pennsylvania. — MILO M. DIMMICK, of Stroudsburg ; JOB MANN, of Bedford ; J. X. McLANAHAN, of Chambersburg ; JOHN ROBBINS, Jr., of Philadelphia ; THOMAS ROSS, of Doylestown ; JAMES THOMPSON, of Erie.

Ohio. — MOSES HOAGLAND, of Millersburg ; JOHN K. MILLER, of Mt. Vernon ; JOHN L. TAYLOR, of Chillicothe.

Michigan. — ALEXANDER W. BUELL, of Detroit.

Indiana. — NATHANIEL ALBERTSON, of Greenville ; WILLIAM J. BROWN, of Amity ; CYRUS L. DUNHAM, of Salem ; WILLIS A. GORMAN, of Bloomington ; JOSEPH E. McDONALD, of Crawfordsville ; EDWARD W McGAUGHEY, of Rockville.

Illinois. — WILLIAM H. BISSELL, of Belleville ; THOMAS L. HARRIS, of Petersburg; JOHN A. McCLERNAND; WILLIAM A. RICHARDSON, of Quincy; TIMOTHY R. YOUNG, of Marshall.

Iowa. — SHEPHERD LEFFLER, of Burlington.

California. — EDWARD GILBERT.

[All these Northern tools of Slavery call themselves *Democrats!* save three — *Eliot*, of Massachusetts, *Taylor*, of Ohio, and *McGaughey*, of Indiana, who were Whigs.]

☞ Every Representative of a slaveholding State, who voted at all, voted YEA. Their names are needless, and are omitted.

NAYS.

Maine. — Otis, Sawtell, Stetson.

New Hampshire. — Amos Tuck.

Vermont. — Hebard, Henry, Meacham.

Massachusetts. — Allen, Duncan, Fowler, Mann.

Rhode Island. — Dixon, King.

Connecticut. — Butler, Booth, Waldo.

New York. — Alexander, Bennett, Briggs, Burrows, Gott, Gould, Halloway, Jackson, John A. King, Preston King, Matteson, McKissock, Nelson, Putnam, Rumsey, Sackett, Schermerhorn, Schoolcraft, Thurman, Underhill, Silvester.

New Jersey. — Hay, King.

Pennsylvania. — Calvin, Chandler, Dickey, Freedley, Hampton, Howe, Moore, Pitman, Reed, Stevens.

Ohio. — Cable, Carter, Campbell, M. B. Corwin, Crowell, Disney, Evans, Giddings, Hunter, Morris, Root, Vinton, Whittlesey, Wood.

Michigan. — Bingham, Sprague.

Indiana. — Fitch, Harlan, Julian, Robinson.
Illinois. — Baker, Wentworth.
Wisconsin. — Cole, Doty, Durkee.
California. — Wright.

ABSENT, OR NOT VOTING.

Andrews, Ashmun (Mass.), Bokee, Brooks, Butler, Casey, Cleveland (Conn.), Clarke, Conger, Duer, Gilmore, Goodenow, Grinnell (Mass.), Levin, Nes, Newell, Ogle, Olds, Peck, Phœnix, Potter, Reynolds, Risley, Rockwell (Mass.), Rose, Schenck, Spaulding, Strong, Sweetser, Thompson (Iowa), Van Dyke, White, Wilmot (Penn.) [33 — all Northern men.]
[Fifteen Southern Representatives did not vote.]

DANIEL WEBSTER was not a member of the Senate when the vote on the Fugitive Slave Bill was taken. He had been made Secretary of State a short time previous. All, however, will remember the powerful aid which he gave to the new compromise measures, and among them to the Fugitive Slave Bill, in his notorious Seventh of March speech, [1850.] A few extracts from that Speech will show how heavily the responsibility for the existence of this Law rests upon DANIEL WEBSTER : —

" I suppose there is to be found no injunction against that relation [slavery] between man and man, in the teachings of the Gospel of Jesus Christ, or of any of his Apostles." — *Webster's 7th March Speech, (authorized edition,)* p. 9.

" One complaint of the South has, in my opinion, just foundation ; and that is, that there has been found at the North, among individuals and among legislators, a disinclination to perform, fully, their Constitutional duties in regard to the return of persons bound to service, who have escaped into the free States. In that respect, it is my judgment that the South is right, and the North is wrong." * * * * " My friend at the head of the Judiciary Committee [Mr. MASON, of Virginia] has a bill on the subject now before the Senate, with some amendments to it, WHICH I PROPOSE TO SUPPORT, WITH ALL ITS PROVISIONS, *to the fullest extent*." — *Idem*, p. 29.

Mr. Webster proceeded to assure the Senate that the North would, on due consideration, fulfil " their constitutional obligations " " *with alacrity.*" " Therefore, I repeat, sir, that here is a ground of complaint against the North well founded, which ought to be removed, which it is now in the power of the different departments of this Government to remove; which calls for the enactment of proper laws authorizing the judicature of this Government, in the several States, to do all that is necessary for the recapture of fugitive slaves, and for the restoration of them to those who claim them. Wherever I go, and whenever I speak on the subject, and when I speak here, I desire to speak to the whole North, I say that the South has been injured in this respect, and has a right to complain; and the North has been too careless of what, I think, the Constitution peremptorily and emphatically enjoins upon her as a duty."—*Idem*, p. 30.

In a speech in the United States Senate, July 17, 1850, made with an evident view to calm that Northern feeling which had been aroused and excited by his 7th of March speech beyond the power of priest or politician wholly to subdue, Mr. WEBSTER said there were various misapprehensions respecting the working of the proposed Fugitive Slave Bill:—

"The first of these misapprehensions," he said, "is an exaggerated sense of the actual evil of the reclamation of fugitive slaves, felt by Massachusetts and the other New England States. What produced that? The cases do not exist. There has not been a case within the knowledge of this generation, in which a man has been taken back from Massachusetts into slavery by process of law—not one." * * * * "Not only has there been no case, so far as I can learn, of the reclamation of a slave by his master, which ended in taking him back to slavery, in this generation, but I will add, that, as far as I have been able to go back in my researches, as far as I have been able to hear and learn, in all that region, there has been no one case of false claim. * * * *There is no danger of any such violation being perpetrated."*—Webster's Speech on the Compromise Bill, in the U. S. Senate, 17th of July, 1850, edition of Gideon & Co., Washington, pp. 23–25.

* See also Mr. Webster's Letter to the Citizens of Newburyport, dated May 15, 1850, wherein he urges the same point, with great pains of argument.

With such words did Mr. Webster endeavor to allay Northern alarm, and to create the impression (which was created, and which prevailed extensively with his friends) that the Fugitive Law was only a concession to Southern feeling, and that few or no attempts to enforce it were likely to be made.

But when a few months had proved him a false prophet, and the Southern chase after fugitive men, women and children had become hot and fierce, and in one or two instances the hunter had been foiled in his attempts, and had lost his prey, Mr. WEBSTER (having become, meantime, Secretary of State, and an aspirant for higher office) changed his tone. In May, 1851, at Syracuse, N. Y., he said:—

"Depend upon it, the Law [the Fugitive Slave Law] will be executed in its spirit and to its letter. It will be executed in all the great cities—here in Syracuse, in the midst of the next Anti-Slavery Convention, if the occasion shall arise."

Certainly, so far as in Mr. Webster lay, so far as was in the power of Mr. Fillmore, and the officers of the United States Government generally, and of the still larger crowd of *expectants* of office, nothing was left undone to introduce the tactics, discipline and customs of the Southern plantation into our Northern cities and towns, in order to enforce the Fugitive Law.

And what the administration of Millard Fillmore, of New York, began, the administrations of Franklin Pierce, of New Hampshire, and of James Buchanan, of Pennsylvania, emulated, and, if possible, surpassed; Whig and Democrat vieing with each other in showing loyalty to the Union, by aiding to sustain this cruel and iniquitous Law. That fearful test question of eighteen centuries ago was asked again of this people and of its government, "Whom will ye that I release unto you? Barabbas, or Jesus which is called Christ?"—CHRIST,

1*

in the person of his little ones, a hungered and athirst, strangers and houseless, or BARABBAS, the robber and the murderer
of these? And the answer came again, as of old, " Not this
man, but BARABBAS!" "Give us our union, our *glorious
union*, with the slaveholder, and as for the slave—crucify
him, crucify him!" Yet, thanks to God for what of justice
and tender compassion were developed in the consciences and
hearts of the people, making them strong to despise the Law
and its penalties, and prompt to succor and save the faint and
flying fugitives! It is our sustaining faith, that, let men
enact and decree what iniquity they please, God will never
leave Himself without a witness in the land, and in the hearts
of the people, against whose monitions and impulses and
availing power the wrath of man will rage in vain.

—————

The remainder of this tract will be devoted to a record, as
complete as circumstances enable us to make, of the VICTIMS
OF THE FUGITIVE SLAVE LAW. It is a terrible record, which
the people of this country should never allow to sleep in
oblivion, until the disgraceful and bloody system of Slavery
is swept from our land, and with it, all Compromise Bills, all
Constitutional Guarantees to Slavery, all Fugitive Slave
Laws. The established and accredited newspapers of the
day, without reference to party distinctions, are the authorities relied upon in making up this record, and the *dates* being
given with each case, the reader is enabled to verify the
same, and the few particulars which the compass of the tract
allows to be given with each. With all the effort which has
been made to secure a good degree of completeness and ex-

actness, the present record must of necessity be an imperfect one, and fall short of exhibiting all the enormities of the Act in question.

JAMES HAMLET, *of New York, September*, 1850, was the first victim. He was surrendered by United States Commissioner Gardiner to the agent of one Mary Brown, of Baltimore, who claimed him as her slave. He was taken to Baltimore. An effort was immediately made to purchase his freedom, and in the existing state of the public feeling, the sum demanded by his mistress, $800, was quickly raised. Hamlet was brought back to New York with great rejoicings.

Near Bedford, Penn., October 1. Ten fugitives, from Virginia, were attacked in Pennsylvania — one mortally wounded, another dangerously. Next morning, both were captured. Five others entered a mountain hut, and begged relief. The woman supplied their wants; her husband went out, procured assistance, captured the slaves, and received a reward of $255.

Harrisburg, Penn., October. Some slaves, number not stated, were brought before Commissioner M'Allister, when " the property was proven, and they were delivered to their masters, who took them back to Virginia, by railroad, without molestation."

Detroit, 8th October. A negro was arrested under the new law, and sent to jail for a week, to await evidence. Great numbers of colored people armed themselves to rescue him. Result not known.

HENRY GARNETT, *Philadelphia*, arrested as the slave of Thomas P. Jones, of Cecil County, Maryland, and taken before Judge Grier, of the United States Supreme Court, October 18, 1850, who declared his determination to execute the law as he found it. The Judge said that the claimant had not taken the course prescribed by the Fugitive Act, and proceeded to explain, in a detailed manner, what the course should be in such cases. As the claimant thus failed to make out his case, the prisoner was ordered to be discharged.

Boston, about 25th October. Attempt to seize WILLIAM and ELLEN CRAFT. William Craft armed himself, and kept within his shop; Ellen was concealed in the house of a friend. Their claimants, named Hughes and Knight, were indicted for defamation of character, in calling W. C. a slave, and brought before a magistrate. The feeling excited against them was so great, that they at length fled from the city. Shortly after, it being considered hazardous for Mr. and Mrs. Craft to remain in the country, they were enabled to escape to England.

[In a letter, dated Macon, Georgia, Nov. 11, John Knight gives a particular account of the proceedings and experiences of himself and his friend Hughes, on their then recent visit to Boston for the purpose, to quote his own language, " of re-capturing William and Ellen Craft, the negroes belonging to Dr. Collins and Ira Taylor." Willis H. Hughes also published his statement.]

New Albany, Indiana. A woman and boy given up, and taken to Louisville. They were so white that, even in Kentucky, a strong feeling arose in their favor on that ground. They were finally bought for $600, and set free.

ADAM GIBSON, *Philadelphia, December* 21, 1850. Surrendered by Edward D. Ingraham, United States Commissioner. The case was hurried through in indecent haste, testimony being admitted against him of the most groundless character. One witness swore that Gibson's name was Emery Rice. He was taken to Elkton, Maryland. There, Mr. William S. Knight, his supposed owner, refused to receive Gibson, saying he was not the man, and he was taken back to Philadelphia.

What compensation has the United States Government ever made to Adam Gibson for the injurious act of its agent, Ingraham? Had not the slaveholder been more honorable than the Commissioner or the makers of the Fugitive Law, Gibson would have been in slavery for life.

HENRY LONG, *New York, December,* 1850. Brought before Commissioner Charles M. Hall, claimed as the fugitive slave of John T. Smith, of Russell County, Virginia. After five or six days' proceedings, there being some doubt of the Commissioner's legal right to act, the alleged fugitive, Long, was taken before Andrew T. Judson,* District Judge of the United States. The Castle Garden Union Safety Committee volunteered their *disinterested* aid, and retained Mr. George Wood in this case, as counsel for the slave claimant! Long was surrendered by Judge Judson, and taken to Richmond, Virginia. Judge J. was complimented by the Washington *Union* as a " clear-headed, competent, and independent officer, who has borne himself with equal discretion, liberality and firmness. Such judges as he," continues the *Union*, " are invaluable in these times of turmoil and agitation." At Richmond, Long was advertised to be sold at public auction. On Saturday, January 18th, he was sold, amid the jeers and scoffs of the spectators, for $750, to David Clapton, of Georgia. The auctioneers, (Pullam & Slade,) in commencing, said there was one condition of the sale : bonds must be given by the purchaser that this man shall be carried South, and that he shall be kept South, and sold, if sold again, to go South ; and they declared their intention to see the terms fully complied with. Long was subsequently advertised for sale at Atlanta, Georgia.

Near Coatsville, Chester County, Penn. On a writ issued by Commissioner Ingraham, Deputy Marshal Halzel and other officers, with the claimant of an alleged fugitive, at night, knocked at the door of a colored family, and asked for a light to enable them to mend their broken harness. The door being opened for this purpose, the marshal's party rushed in, and said they came to arrest a fugitive slave. Resistance was made by the occupant of the house and others, and the marshal's party finally driven off—the slave owner advising that course, and saying, "Well, if this is a specimen of the pluck of Pennsylvania negroes, I do n't want my slaves back." The master of the house was severely wounded in the arm by a pistol shot ; still he maintained his ground, declaring the marshal's party should not pass except by first taking his life.

---

* Notorious for being the leader of the mob which broke up Miss Crandall's school for colored girls in Canterbury, Ct.

Marion, Williamson County, Illinois, about December 10, 1850. Mr. O'Havre, of the city police, Memphis, Tennessee, arrested and took back to Memphis a fugitive slave, belonging to Dr. Young. He did so, as the Memphis paper states, only "after much difficulty and heavy expense," being strongly opposed by the Free Soilers and Abolitionists, but "was assisted by Mr. W. Allen, Member of Congress, and other gentlemen."

Philadelphia, about January 10, 1851. G. F. Alberti and others seized, under the Fugitive Slave Law, a free colored boy, named JOEL THOMPSON, alleging that he was a slave. The boy was saved.

STEPHEN BENNETT, *Columbia, Penn.*, arrested as the slave of Edward B. Gallup, of Baltimore. Taken before Commissioner Ingraham; thence, by *habeas corpus*, before Judge Kane. He was saved only by his freedom being purchased by his friends.

The Huntsville (Ala.) Advocate of January 1, 1851, said that Messrs. Markwood & Chester had brought back "*seven of their slaves*" from Michigan.

The Memphis (Tenn.) Eagle, of a later date, says that within a few weeks, "at least five fugitive slaves have been brought back to this city, from free States, with as little trouble as would be had in recovering stray cows." The same paper adds, "We occasionally receive letters notifying us that a slave, said to be the property of some one in this vicinity, has been lodged in jail in Illinois or Indiana, for his owner, who will please call, pay charges, and take him away."

Mrs. TAMOR, or EUPHEMIA WILLIAMS, *Philadelphia, February*, 1851, mother of six children, arrested and brought before Commissioner Ingraham, as the slave Mahala, belonging to William T. J. Purnell, of Worcester County, Maryland, admitted to have been absent since 1829 — twenty-two years. Children all born in Pennsylvania; oldest about seventeen — a girl. Her husband also in custody, and alleged to be the slave of another man. Under writ of *habeas corpus*, Mrs. Williams was taken before Judge Kane, of the United States Circuit Court. After a full hearing, she was discharged, as not being the woman alleged.

SHADRACH, *in Boston, February* 15, 1851. Arrested in Taft's Cornhill Coffee House, by deputies of United States Marshal Devens, on a warrant issued by George T. Curtis, United States Commissioner, on the complaint of John Caphart, attorney of John De Bree, of Norfolk, Va. Seth J. Thomas appeared as counsel for Caphart. After a brief hearing before G. T. Curtis, Commissioner, the case was adjourned to the following Tuesday. Shortly after the adjournment, the court-room was entered by a body of men, who bore away the prisoner, Shadrach; after which, he was heard of in Montreal, Canada, having successfully, with the aid of many friends, escaped the snares of all kidnappers, in and out of Boston. The acting President, MILLARD FILLMORE, issued his proclamation, countersigned by DANIEL WEBSTER, Secretary of State, requiring prosecutions to be commenced against all who participated in the rescue. A series of annoying and irritating "rescue trials" followed.

Shawneetown, Ill. A woman was claimed by Mr. Haley, of Georgia, as his slave; and was delivered up to him by two Justices of the Peace, (early in 1851.)

Madison, Indiana. George W. Mason, of Davies County, Ky., arrested a colored man, named MITCHUM, who, with his wife and children, lived near Vernon. The case was tried before a Justice of the Peace, named Basnett, who was satisfied that Mitchum was Davis's slave, and had left his service *nineteen years before.* The slave was accordingly delivered up, and was taken to Kentucky, (Feb. 1851.)

Clearfield County, Penn., about 20*th January*, 1851. A boy was kidnapped and taken into slavery. — *Mercer (Penn.) Presbyterian.*

Near Ripley, Ohio. A fugitive slave, about January 20, killed his pursuer. He was afterwards taken and carried back to slavery.

Burlington, Lawrence County, Ohio, near the end of February, 1851, four liberated slaves were kidnapped, re-enslaved, and sold. Efforts were made to bring the perpetrators of this nefarious act to punishment, and restore the victims to freedom.

At Philadelphia, early in March, 1851, occurred the case of the colored woman HELEN or HANNAH, and her son, a child of tender years. She was taken before a Commissioner, and thence, by writ of *habeas corpus,* before Judge Kane. An additional question arose from the fact that the woman would soon become the mother of another child. Judge Kane decided that she was the property of John Perdu, of Baltimore, together with her son, *and her unborn child,* and they were all surrendered accordingly, and taken into slavery.

Pittsburg, March 13, 1851. RICHARD GARDINER was arrested in Bridgewater, Beaver County, Pennsylvania, claimed as the property of Miss R. Byers, of Louisville, Ky. Judge Irwin, of the United States District Court, " remanded the fugitive back to his owner." He was afterwards bought for $600, and brought into a free State.

The Wilmington (Del.) Journal, in March, 1851, says kidnapping has become quite frequent in that State, and speaks of a negro kidnapped in that city, on the previous Wednesday night, by a man who had been one of the city watchmen.

THOMAS SIMS, arrested in *Boston,* April 4, 1851, at first on pretence of a charge of theft; but when he understood it was as a fugitive from slavery, he drew a knife and wounded one of the officers. He was taken before Commissioner George T. Curtis. To guard against a repetition of the Shadrach rescue, the United States Marshal, Devens, aided by the Mayor (John P. Bigelow) and City Marshal (Francis Tukey) of Boston, surrounded the Court House, in Boston, with heavy chains, guarded it by an extra force of police officers, with a body of guards also within the building, *where the fugitive was imprisoned* as well as tried. Several military companies, also, were called out by the city authorities, and kept in readiness night and day to act against the people, should they attempt the deliverance of Sims; Faneuil Hall itself being turned into barracks for these hirelings of slavery. Every effort was made by S. E. Sewall, Esq., Hon. Robert Rantoul, Jr., and Charles G. Loring, Esq., to save Sims from being returned into slavery, and Boston from the eternal and ineffaceable disgrace of the act. But in vain.

The omnipotent Slave Power demanded of Boston a victim for its infernal sacrifices. Millard Fillmore, Daniel Webster, and their numerous tools, on the Bench, in Commissioners' seats, and other official stations, or in hopes of gaining such stations bye and bye, had fallen upon their faces before the monster idol, and sworn that the victim should be prepared. Thomas Sims was ordered back to slavery by Commissioner George T. Curtis, and was taken from the Court House, in Boston, early on the morning of April 11th, [1851,] to the brig Acorn, lying at the end of Long Wharf, and thence, in the custody of officers, to Savannah, Georgia. There, after being lodged in jail, and severely and cruelly whipped, as was reported, he was at length sold, and became merged and lost in the great multitude of the enslaved population. The surrender of Sims is said to have cost the United States Government $10,000; the city of Boston about as much more; and Mr. Potter, the claimant of Sims, about $2,400,—making a total of some $22,000, directly expended on the case.

On this subject of the cost of recovering fugitive slaves, and especially in this case, read the following from the *Macon* (Georgia) *Journal*, which was also copied approvingly by the *Nashville* (Tennessee) *Whig:* —

"Some of the papers even pretend that Mr. Potter was compelled to pay all, or nearly all, of the costs and charges in the case of Sims. This is not the fact. Every item of the necessary expenses, incident to the return, was paid by the General Government, as required by law. It even paid the expenses of the half dozen police officers who guarded him to Savannah. When Messrs. Bacon and De Lyon, the agents, applied to Seth Thomas, Esq., their attorney, to know the amount of his fee, his reply was that it had been settled by the people of Boston. The truth is, that it costs the owner less, in many respects, to reclaim a runaway under the late law, than it would to recover one from Kentucky ; because he gets rid of many expenses at the North which are necessarily incurred at the South, and under our own laws."

Vincennes, Indiana, April, 1851. Four fugitive slaves were seized, claimed by one Mr. Kirwan, of or near Florence, Alabama. The magistrate, named Robinson, gave up the fugitives, and they were taken into slavery.

MOSES JOHNSON, *Chicago, Illinois,* brought before a United States Commissioner, and discharged as not answering to the description of the man claimed.

In Salisbury Township, Penn., April, 1851, an elderly man was kidnapped and carried into Maryland.

Near Sandy Hill, Chester County, Penn., in March, 1851, a very worthy and estimable colored man, named Thomas Hall, was forcibly seized, his house being broken into by three armed ruffians, who beat him and his wife with clubs. He was kidnapped.

CHARLES WEDLEY, kidnapped from Pittsburg, Penn., and taken into Maryland. He was found, and brought back.

Cincinnati, Ohio, June 3, 1851, an attempt to arrest a fugitive was made; but a scuffle ensued, in which the man escaped.

Cincinnati, Ohio. About the same time, some slaves, (number not stated,) belonging to Rev. Mr. Perry and others, of Covington, Ky., were taken in Cincinnati, and carried back to Kentucky.

Philadelphia, end of June, 1851, a colored man was taken away as a slave, by steamboat. A writ of *habeas corpus* was got out, but the officer could not find the man. This is probably the same case with that of JESSE WHITMAN, arrested at Wilkesbarre.

FRANK JACKSON, a free colored man in *Mercer, Penn.,* was taken, early in 1851, by a man named Charles May, into Virginia, and sold as a slave. He tried to escape, but was taken and lodged in Fincastle jail, Virginia.

THOMAS SCOTT JOHNSON, free colored man, of *New Bedford, Mass.,* was arrested near Portsmouth, Virginia, and was about to be sold as a slave; but, by the strenuous interposition of Capt. Card, certificates were obtained from New Bedford, and he was set at liberty.

ELIZABETH WILLIAMS, *West Chester County, Penn.,* delivered into slavery by Commissioner Jones. (July, 1851.)

DANIEL HAWKINS, of *Lancaster County, Penn.,* (July, 1851,) was brought before Commissioner Ingraham, Philadelphia, and by him delivered to his claimant, and he was taken into slavery.

New Athens, Ohio, July 8, 1851. Eighteen slaves, who had escaped from Lewis County, Ky., were discovered in an old building in Adams County, Ohio. Some white men, professing to be friendly, misled them, and brought them to a house, where they were imprisoned, bound one by one, and carried back to Kentucky. [The enactment of the Fugitive Slave Law is the direct stimulating cause of all these cases of kidnapping.]

Buffalo, August, 1851. Case of DANIEL ——. D. was a cook on board the steamer "Buckeye State." He was engaged in his avocation, when Benj. S. Rust, with a warrant from United States Commissioner H. K. Smith, went on board the boat. Daniel was called up from below, and as his head appeared above the deck, Rust struck him a heavy blow, upon the head, with a large billet of wood, which knocked him back into the cook-room, where he fell upon the stove, and was badly burned. In this state, he was brought before the Commissioner, "bleeding profusely at the back of the head, and at the nose, and was, moreover, so stupefied by the assault, that he fell asleep several times during the brief and very summary proceedings." For most of the time, he was unable to converse with his counsel, and "sat dozing, with the blood slowly oozing out of his mouth and nostrils." After a very hurried form and mockery of a trial, Daniel was ordered to be delivered to Rust, the agent of George H. Moore, of Louisville, Kentucky. By a writ of *habeas corpus*, Daniel was brought before Judge Conkling, of the United States Court, at Auburn, who gave a decision that set Daniel at liberty, and he was immediately hurried by his friends into Canada. Rust was indicted, in Buffalo, for his brutal assault on Daniel. It was fully proved; he afterwards plead guilty, and was let off with the paltry fine of fifty dollars.

JOHN BOLDING, *arrested in Poughkeepsie, N. Y.*, claimed as the property of Barret Anderson, of Columbia, S. C. Bolding was a young man, of good character, recently married, and had a small tailor's shop in P. He said he was told, when he was a boy, that he was the son of a white man. He was tried before United States Commissioner Nelson, who ordered him to be delivered up to his claimants, and he was taken quietly from the city to Columbia, S. C. The sum of

$2,000 was raised in New York, and paid to Bolding's owner, who had consented to take that sum for him, and Bolding returned to his family in Poughkeepsie.

Christiana, Lancaster County, Penn., Sept., 1851. Edward Gorsuch, (represented as a very pious member of a Methodist Church in Baltimore!) with his son Dickinson, accompanied by the Sheriff of Lancaster County, Penn., and by a Phi'adelphia officer named *Henry Kline*, went to Christiana to arrest certain slaves of his, who (as he had been privately informed by a wretch named Wm. M. Padgett) were living there. An attack was made upon the house, the slaveholder declaring (as was said) that he "would not leave the place alive without his slaves." "Then," replied one of them, "you will not leave here alive." Many shots were fired on both sides, and the slave-hunter, Edward Gorsuch, was killed.

At a subsequent trial, a number of persons (nearly forty) were committed to take their trial for "treason against the United States, by levying war against the same, in resisting by force of arms the execution of the Fugitive Slave Law." CASTNER HANWAY was of the number. After suffering imprisonment, and being subjected to great loss of time and heavy expenses, they were all discharged.

Syracuse, October 1, 1851. JERRY, claimed as the slave of John McReynolds, of Marion County, Missouri, was brought to trial before Commissioner J. F. Sabine. He was rescued by a large body of men from the officers who had him in custody, and was next heard of in Canada.

James R. Lawrence, a lawyer of Syracuse, acted as counsel for *James Lear*, attorney of McReynolds.

[N. B. Daniel Webster's prophecy (see page 9) was not fulfilled.]

Columbia, Penn., (fall of 1851.) Man named HENRY, arrested as the slave of Dr. Duvall, of Prince George's County, Maryland; taken to Harrisburg, before United States Commissioner M'Allister, and by him consigned to slavery.

JUDGE DENNING, of Illinois, discharged a negro brought before him as a fugitive slave, on the ground that the Fugitive Slave Law was unconstitutional.

Two alleged slaves arrested at Columbia, Penn., on warrant of United States Commissioner M'Allister,—claimed as property of W. T. McDermott, of Baltimore. One was carried into slavery; one escaped. (November, 1851.)

Near New Philadelphia, Maryland, a woman, married to a free colored man, with whom she had lived ten years, was arrested as the slave of a Mr. Shreve, of Louisville, Ky. She was taken back to Kentucky.

RACHEL PARKER, free colored girl, kidnapped from house of Joseph S. Miller, West Nottingham, Penn., by the "notorious Elkton Kidnapper, McCreary," Dec. 31, 1851. Mr. Miller tracked the kidnappers to Baltimore, and tried to recover the girl, but in vain. On his way home, he was induced to leave the cars, and was undoubtedly murdered — it was supposed, in revenge for the death of Gorsuch, at Christiana. Mr. Miller's body was found suspended from a tree. A suit was brought in the Circuit Court of Baltimore County, for the freedom of Rachel Parker, Jan., 1853. Over sixty witnesses, from Pennsylvania, attended to testify to her being free-born, and that she was not the person she was claimed to be; although, in great bodily terror, she had, after her capture, confessed herself the alleged slave! So complete and strong was the evidence in her favor, that, after an eight days' trial, the claimants abandoned the case, and a verdict was rendered for the freedom of Rachel, and also of her sister, Elizabeth Parker, who had been previously kidnapped, and conveyed to New Orleans.

☞ McCreary was demanded by Gov. Bigler, of Pennsylvania, to be delivered up for trial on a charge of kidnapping; but Gov. Lowe, of Maryland, refused to surrender him. See *National Anti-Slavery Standard*, July 2, 1853.

JAMES TASKER, *New York City*, (Feb., 1852,) arrested through the treachery of Police Officer Martin, and brought before United States Commissioner George W. Morton, as the slave of Jonathan Pinckney, of Maryland. He was given up, and taken back to slavery.

HORACE PRESTON, arrested in *Williamsburg, New York*, as the slave of William Reese, of Baltimore, Maryland—Rich-

ard Busteed, of New York, being attorney for the slaveholder. He was brought before United States Commissioner
Morton, 1st April, 1852 ; for several days previous, he had
been kept a prisoner, and his wife knew not what had become
of him. He was given up by the Commissioner, and was
carried into slavery. The same policeman, Martin, who acted in the case of James Tasker, was active also in this case ;
being, doubtless, the original informant.

Preston was afterwards bought for about $1,200, and
brought back.

Columbia, Penn., (end of March, 1852 ;) a colored man,
named WILLIAM SMITH, was arrested as a fugitive slave in the
lumber yard of Mr. Gottlieb, by Deputy Marshal Snyder, of
Harrisburg, and Police Officer Ridgeley, of Baltimore, under
a warrant from Commissioner M'Allister. Smith endeavored
to escape, when Ridgeley drew a pistol, and shot him dead !
Ridgeley was demanded by the Governor of Pennsylvania, of
the Governor of Maryland, and the demand was referred to
the Maryland Legislature.

Hon. J. R. Giddings proposed the erection of a monument
to Smith.

JAMES PHILLIPS, who had resided in *Harrisburg, Penn.*,
for fourteen years, was arrested May 24, 1852, as the former
slave of Dennis Hudson, of Culpepper County, Virginia, afterwards bought by Henry T. Fant, of Fauquier County. He
was brought before United States Commissioner M'Allister.
Judge McKinney volunteered his services to defend the alleged fugitive. The Commissioner, as soon as possible, ordered the man to be delivered up ; and, after fourteen years'
liberty, he was taken back to slavery, in Virginia. Afterwards, bought for $900, and taken back to Harrisburg.

Wilkesbarre, Penn., (summer of 1852.)   Mr. Harvey arrested and fined, for shielding a slave.

Sacramento, California ; a man named Lathrop claimed
another as his slave, and Judge Fry decided that the claim
was good, and ordered the slave to be surrendered. Mr.
Lathrop left, with his slave, for the Atlantic States.

A beautiful young woman, nearly white, was pursued by
her owner [and father] to New York, (end of June, 1852.)

There a large reward was offered to a police officer to discover her place of residence. It was discovered, and measures taken for her apprehension; but the alarm had been taken, and she escaped.

Sacramento, California ; three men were seized by a Mr. Perkins, of Mississippi. The Court decided them to be his property, and they were carried back to Mississippi.—*Standard,* July 29, 1852.

Petersburg, Penn. Two fugitives from Alabama slavery were overtaken, and taken back, September, 1852.

JOHN HENRY WILSON, a lad of fourteen years, kidnapped from Danville, Penn., and taken to Baltimore, where he was offered for sale to John N. Deming. Kidnappers committed to jail, October, 1852.

[☞ DANIEL WEBSTER, the endorser of the Fugitive Slave Law, died at Marshfield, Mass., October 24th, 1852, in the very height of the Law's triumphant operation.]

LOUISA, a colored woman, claimed by Mrs. Reese, of San Francisco, Cal., was seized by five armed men, and put on board Steamer Golden Gate, and carried, it is not known whither. The aid of the Law was not invoked. The California *Christian Advocate,* from which the above is taken, says : — " Two colored men, stewards on the Golden Gate, were sent back to the States on the last trip, under the State Fugitive Law."

A mulatto woman, in San Francisco, was ordered to be delivered to her claimant, T. T. Smith, Jackson County, Mo., by " Justice Shepherd."— *San Francisco Herald*— in *Standard,* November 4, 1852.

Sandusky, Ohio. Two men, two women, and several children were arrested, and taken from a steamboat just about to leave for Detroit. Taken before Mayor Follett, by a man who claimed to be their owner. R. R. Sloane, Esq., was employed as counsel for the slaves. No one claiming custody of the slaves, or producing any writs or warrants, Mr. Sloane signified to the crowd present that there appeared to be no cause for the detention of the persons. Immediately a rush was made for the door. A man, who before had been silent, exclaimed : — "Here are the papers — I own the slaves — I'll hold you individually responsible for their escape." The slaves escaped into Canada, October, 1852. Mr. Sloane was afterwards prosecuted for the value of the slaves, and judgment given against him, to the amount of $3,950.

" *Thirty slaves*," says the Maysville (Ky.) *Eagle*, " escaped from Mason and Bracken Counties, a short time ago. Some of them were captured in Ohio, by their owners, at a distance of about forty miles from the river." " They brought the captured slaves home without encountering the least obstacle, or even an unkind word." — *Standard, November* 4, 1852.

THE LEMMON SLAVES. At New York, eight persons, claimed by Jonathan Lemmon, of Norfolk, Va., as his slaves, were brought before Judge Paine, November, 1852. It appeared that they had been brought to New York by their owner, with a view of taking them to Texas, as his slaves. Mr. Louis Napoleon, a respectable colored man, of New York, procured a writ of *habeas corpus*, under which they were brought before the Court. Their liberation was called for, under the State law, not being fugitives, but brought into a free State by their owner. Said owner appeared, with Henry D. Lapaugh as his counsel, aided by Mr. Clinton. At their urgent request, the case was postponed from time to time, when Judge Paine decreed the freedom of the slaves. E. D. Culver and John Jay, Esqs., were counsel for the slaves. The merchants and others of New York subscribed and paid Mr. Lemmon the sum of $5,280, for loss of his slaves. The New York *Journal of Commerce* was very active in raising this money. The same men were invited to contribute something for the destitute men, women and children claimed by Lemmon. The whole amount given by them all was two dollars. About one thousand dollars were raised for them among the better disposed, but less wealthy class. In October, 1857, the case being still before the Supreme Court of New York, John Jay, Esq., moved the Court that the case be dismissed, inasmuch as the plaintiffs, the Lemmons, really had no interest at stake, they having been fully remunerated for the loss of their slaves, by a public subscription. The Court gave a decision, affirming the original decision of Judge Paine, which declared the slaves free. See *Standard*, December 12, 1857.

THOMAS BROWN, *alias* GEORGE BORDLEY, *Philadelphia*, November, 1852, was claimed by one Andrew Pearce, Cecil County, Md. Given up to claimant by Commissioner Ingraham. The arrest of the man was made by the notorious kidnapper, George F. Alberti. Mr. Pettit, counsel for the claimant.

RICHARD NEAL, free colored man, kidnapped in Philadelphia, and carried from the city in a carriage, towards Maryland. A writ of *habeas corpus* was obtained, the kidnappers were overtaken, and Neal brought back, after resistance and various hindrances. The Supreme Court of Pennsylvania discharged him. February, 1853.

Ten slaves, arrested in Indiana, and taken back to Tennessee, by W. Carney and others. Resistance was made, and W. Carney " was very badly injured during the fracas." — *Nashville Whig*, March 5, 1853.

Alton, Illinois. A man claimed to belong to Walter Carrico, of Warren County, Mo., was arrested by police officers from St. Louis. After being lodged in jail in St. Louis, he made his escape, and again went into Illinois. He was pursued, found, and taken back to St. Louis. — *St. Louis Republican*, March, 1853.

AMANDA, a slave girl, was brought to St. Louis, from near Memphis, Tenn., a year before, by a son of her master, and by him set free, without his father's consent. After the father's death, an attempt was made to seize Amanda, and take her back to Tennessee, without trial. This was prevented by officers, the girl taken from the steamboat Cornelia, and brought before Levi Davis, United States Commissioner. He decided in favor of the claimants, (the heirs of the estate, of course.) — *St. Louis Republican*, March 17, 1853.

JANE TRAINER, a colored child, about ten years old, in the possession of Mrs. Rose Cooper, *alias* Porter, (a woman admitted by her counsel to be a common prostitute,) was brought before Judge Duer, of New York City, by a writ of *habeas corpus*, which had been applied for by Charles Trainer, the father of the child, (a free colored man, who had followed the parties from Mobile to New York,) and who desired that the custody of his daughter's person should be granted to him.

2

[June, 1853, and previous.] Judge Duer decided that it was not within his jurisdiction to determine to whom the custody of the child belonged ; the Supreme Court of New York must decide that. Judge D. proposed to both parties that the child should be put into his hands, and he would provide a proper person for her care and education, but the woman (Porter) would not consent to this. She evidently designed to train up the child for a life of shame, and perhaps of slavery also. The case was brought by a writ of *habeas corpus* before Judge Barculo, of the Supreme Court, sitting at Brooklyn. The effort to serve the writ was at first defeated by the notorious New York bully, Captain Isaiah Rynders, acting, it was said, under the advice of James T. Brady, counsel for Mrs. Porter. For this interference with the law, Rynders and some others were arrested and taken before Judge Barculo, who let them off on their making an apology ! The second attempt to serve the writ on the child was more successful. After hearing counsel, Judge Barculo adjudged " that the said Charles Trainer is entitled to the care and custody of said Jane Trainer, and directing her to be delivered to him as her father," &c. In giving his decision, Judge B. said : — " It is not to be assumed that a child under fourteen years of age is possessed of sufficient discretion to choose her own guardian ; a house of ill-fame is not a suitable place, nor one of its inmates a proper person, for the education of such a child." Jane Trainer's mother was afterwards bought from slavery in Mobile, Ala., and enabled to join her husband and child.

In 1854, Charles Trainer obtained a verdict in King's County Court, N. Y., for $775 damages, against Rose Cooper.

[N. B. Though not strictly a case under the Fugitive Slave Law, this is very properly inserted here, as the whole spirit of the woman, of her counsel, and of the means he took to accomplish his base designs, was clearly instigated by that Law, and by the malignant influences it brought into action against the colored people, both slave and free.]

Two slaves of Sylvester Singleton, living near Burlington, (Ky. ?) escaped and reached Columbus, Ohio ; were there overtaken by their master, who secured them, and took them back with him. — *Cincinnati Enquirer*.

BASIL WHITE, Philadelphia, was summarily surrendered into slavery in Maryland, by United States Commissioner Ingraham, June 1, 1853. He was betrayed into the clutches of the kidnapper Alberti by a colored man named John Dorsey.

JOHN FREEMAN, a free colored man, seized in Indianapolis, and claimed as the slave of Pleasant Ellington, a Methodist church-member, (summer, 1853,) of Missouri. Freeman pledged himself to prove that he was not the person he was alleged to be. The United States Marshal consented to his having time for this, provided he would go to jail, and pay *three dollars a day* for a guard to keep him secure! Bonds to any amount, to secure the Marshal against loss, if Freeman could go at large, were rejected. Freeman's counsel went to Georgia, and "after many days, returned with a venerable and highly respectable gentleman from Georgia, Mr. Patillo, (postmaster of the place where he resides,) who voluntarily made the long journey for the sole purpose of testifying to his knowledge of Freeman, and that he was well known to be free!" But Freeman was still kept in jail. After several days, Ellington brought witnesses to prove F. to be his slave. The witnesses and Liston, (counsel for Ellington,) wished to have Freeman strip himself, to be examined naked. By advice of his counsel, he refused. The Marshal took him to his cell, and compelled him to strip. The witnesses then swore that he was Ellington's property. Freeman's counsel produced further evidence that he had been known as a free man *twenty* years. Ellington claimed that he had escaped from him *sixteen* years before. The man who did escape from Ellington, just sixteen years before, was discovered to be living near Malden, Canada. Two of the Kentucky witnesses visited and recognized him. Freeman was then released, but with a large debt upon him, $1,200, which had grown up by the unusually heavy expenses of his defence and long imprisonment. Freeman brought a suit against Ellington for false imprisonment, laying damages at $10,000. A verdict for $2,000 was given in his favor, which was agreed to by Ellington's counsel. — *Indiana Free Democrat*, May, 1854.

Three slaves, two men and a girl, fled from near Maysville, Ky., into Ohio. Were pursued by their owners and assis-

tants, five men armed, and were overtaken, says the Maysville
Weekly Express, "at the bridge over Rattlesnake Creek, on
the Petersburg and Greenfield road, about ten o'clock at
night," the slaves being armed, and accompanied by a white
man. Both parties fired, the negro girl was wounded, but
still fled; one of the negro men was also wounded, "and,"
says the Maysville paper, they "were tracked a mile and a
half by the blood." The other slave was secured and taken
back to Kentucky, "much bruised and cut in the affray."
"The white man," says the same paper, "was also caught
and beaten in a very severe manner with a club, and strong
hopes are entertained that he will die."— *Wilmington (Ohio)
Republican*, July 22, 1853.

A colored girl, between four and five years old, suddenly
disappeared from Providence, R. I., July 13, 1853; at the
same time, a mulatto woman, who had been heard to make
inquiries about the child, was missing also. Believed to be
a case of kidnapping.

A negro boy, says the Memphis *Inquirer*, "left his owner
in this city," and went on board the steamboat Aurilla Wood,
bound for Cincinnati. By a telegraphic message he was intercepted, taken from the boat at Cairo, Ill., and taken back
to Memphis. (Summer, 1853.)

GEORGE WASHINGTON McQUERRY, *Cincinnati, Ohio.* A
colored man, who had resided three or four years in Ohio, and
married a free woman, by whom he had three children. was
remanded to slavery by Judge John McLean, (August, 1853.)
The man was taken by the United States Marshal, with a
posse, across the river to Covington, Ky., and there delivered
to his *master !* Judge McLean, in his decision, pronounced
the Fugitive Slave Law to be constitutional.

Two men kidnapped from Chicago, and taken to St. Louis.
See Chicago *Tribune*, quoted in *Standard*, August 27, 1853.

Three slaves taken by *habeas corpus* from steamboat Tropic,
and brought before Judge Flinn, at Cincinnati, August, 1853.
The woman Hannah expressed a wish to return to her master
in the boat. Judge Flinn ordered her into the custody of the
claimants, without investigation. Judge F. asked Hannah if
she had the custody of the child Susan, to which she an-

swered that she had. Whereupon the Judge also ordered her back into the custody of the claimants, without examination. Mr. Jolliffe protested against ordering the child back without examination. The Court said it would take the responsibility. The examination then proceeded in the case of the man Edward. It appeared that they were purchased in Virginia, to be conveyed to Mississippi. The boat stopped at Cincinnati, and the slaves were twice taken by the agent of the owners on shore, and upon the territory of Ohio. Mr. Jolliffe commenced his argument at 7, P. M., and argued that the slaves, being brought by their owners upon free territory, were legally free. Mr. J., before finishing, was taken ill, and obliged to leave the court-room; he first begged the Court to adjourn until morning, which was refused by Judge Flinn. Judge Keys said the Ohio river was a highway for all States bordering on it, whose citizens had a right also to use the adjacent shores for purposes necessary to navigation. Mr. Zinn stated that Mr. Jolliffe had been obliged to retire, in consequence of illness, and had requested him to urge the Court to continue the case. Judge Flinn said—"The case will be decided to-night; that is decided on. We have not been sitting here four or five hours to determine whether we will decide the case or not. It will be decided, and you may come up to it sideways or square, or any way you please; you must come to it." Mr. Zinn said he was not going to argue. He had made the request out of courtesy to a professional brother. He doubted the power of the Court to deliver the boy into slavery. Judge Flinn said—"I do not wish to hear any arguments of that nature." The man was then ordered to be taken by the Sheriff, and delivered to claimant on board the boat—which was done.—*Cincinnati Gazette*, 27th August, 1853.

PATRICK SNEED, a colored waiter in the Cataract House, Niagara Falls, arrested on the pretended charge of murder committed in Savannah, Georgia. He was brought, by *habeas corpus*, before Judge Sheldon, at Buffalo, (September, 1853,) and by him ordered to be "fully discharged."

BILL, [or WILLIAM THOMAS,] a colored waiter at the Phœnix Hotel, Wilkesbarre, Penn., described as a "tall, noble-looking, intelligent, and active mulatto, nearly white," was attacked by "Deputy Marshal Wynkoop," Sept. 3, 1853, and four other persons, (three of them from Virginia.) These men came "suddenly, from behind, knocked him down with a mace, and partially shackled him." He struggled hard against the five, shook them off, and with the handcuff, which had been secured to his right wrist only, "inflicted some hard wounds on the countenances" of his assailants. Covered with blood, he broke from them, rushed from the house, and plunged in the river close by, exclaiming, "I will be drowned rather than taken alive." He was pursued, fired upon repeatedly, ordered to come out of the water, where he stood immersed to his neck, or "they would blow his brains out." He replied, "I will die first." They then deliberately fired at him four or five different times, the last ball supposed to have struck on his head, for his face was instantly covered with blood, and he sprang up and shrieked. The bystanders began to cry shame, and the kidnappers retired a short distance for consultation. Bill came out of the water and lay down on the shore. His pursuers, supposing him dying, said, "Dead niggers are not worth taking South." Some one brought and put on him a pair of pantaloons. He was helped to his feet by a colored man named Rex; on seeing which, Wynkoop and party headed him and presented their revolvers, when Bill again ran into the river, "where he remained upwards of an hour, nothing but his head above water, covered with blood, and in full view of hundreds who lined the banks." His claimants dared not follow him into the water, for, as he said afterward, "he would have died contented, could he have carried two or three of them down with him." Preparations [rather slow, it would appear!] were made to arrest the murderous gang, but they had departed from the place. Bill then waded some distance up the stream, and "was found by some women flat on his face in a corn-field. They carried him to a place of safety, dressed his wounds," and the suffering man was seen no more in Wilkesbarre.— *Correspondence of New York Tribune.*

Wynkoop and another were afterwards arrested in Philadelphia, on a charge of riot, the warrant issuing from a State magistrate of Wilkesbarre, on the complaint of William C. Gildersleeve, of that place. Mr. Jackson, the constable who held them in custody, was brought before Judge Grier, of the

United States Supreme Court, by *habeas corpus*. Judge Grier, during the examination, said:—

"I will not have the officers of the United States harassed at every step in the performance of their duties by every petty magistrate who chooses to harass them, or by any unprincipled interloper who chooses to make complaints against them—for I know something of the man who makes this complaint." "If this man Gildersleeve fails to make out the facts set forth in the warrant of arrest, I will request the Prosecuting Attorney of Luzerne County to prosecute him for perjury. * * * If any tuppenny magistrate, or any unprincipled interloper can come in, and cause to be arrested the officers of the United States, whenever they please, it is a sad affair. * * * If *habeas corpuses* are to be taken out after that manner, I will have an indictment sent to the United States Grand Jury against the person who applies for the writ, or assists in getting it, the lawyer who defends it, and the sheriff who serves the writ. * * * I will see that my officers are protected."

On a subsequent day, Judge Grier gave an elaborate opinion, reciting the facts in the case, *as stated by the prisoners*, and ordering them to be *discharged!* He said:—

"We are unable to perceive, in this transaction, any thing worthy of blame in the conduct of these officers, in their unsuccessful endeavors to fulfil a most dangerous and disgusting duty; except, perhaps, a want of sufficient courage and perseverance in the attempt to execute the writ"!

Wynkoop and the other were discharged by Judge Kane, on the ground that they did only what their duty, under the Law, required. (May, 1854.)

A family of colored persons, at Uniontown, Pa., were claimed as slaves by a man in Virginia. They admitted that they had been his slaves, but declared that they had come into Pennsylvania with their master's consent and knowledge, on a visit to some friends in Fayette County, and were not, therefore, *fugitives*. This was overruled, and the negroes were sent back by a United States Commissioner, name not given. (September, 1853.)—*Pittsburg Saturday Visiter.*

A desperate fight between a party of four fugitives and about double the number of whites, took place in Carroll County, Maryland. Four white men shot—none dangerously. Two of the slaves wounded, one severely. They were captured. (October, 1853.) — *Westminster (Md.) Democrat.*

Washington, Indiana. In April, 1853, GEORGE, a negro man, was arrested and claimed by a Mr. Rice, of Kentucky, as his slave. Judge Clemens ordered his surrender to Rice, who took him to Louisville, and there sold him to a slave-trader, who took him to Memphis, Tenn. Here a man from Mississippi claimed that George was *his* slave, obtained a writ of replevin, and took possession of him.

JOSHUA GLOVER, colored man, claimed as the slave of B. S. Garland, of St. Louis County, Missouri, was arrested near Racine, Wisconsin, about the 10th of March, 1854. Arrest made by five men, who burst suddenly into his shanty, put a pistol to his head, felled him to the ground, handcuffed him, and took him in a wagon to Milwaukee jail, a distance of twenty-five miles. They swore that if he shouted or made the least noise, they would kill him instantly. When visited, says the Milwaukee *Sentinel*, "We found him in his cell. He was cut in two places on the head; the front of his shirt and vest were soaking and stiff with his own blood." A writ of *habeas corpus* was immediately issued; also a warrant for the arrest of the five men who assaulted and beat him in his shanty. Thousands of people collected around the jail and Court House, "the excitement being intense." A vigilance committee of twenty-five persons was appointed to watch the jail at night, and see that Glover was not secretly taken away. The next day, at about five o'clock, P. M., a considerable accession of persons being made to the crowd, and it appearing that every attempt to save Glover by the laws of Wisconsin had been overruled by United States Judge Miller, a demand was made for the man. This being refused, an attack was made upon the door with axes, planks, &c. It was broken in, the inner door and wall broken through, and Glover taken from his keepers, brought out, placed in a wagon, and driven off at great speed.

S. M. Booth, editor of the *Milwaukee Free Democrat*, Charles Clement, of the *Racine Advocate*, W. H. Waterman, and George S. Wright, were arrested for aiding and abetting the rescue of Glover. Booth was subsequently discharged by the Supreme Court of Wisconsin, on the ground that the Fugitive Slave Law is unconstitutional. He was, however, re-arrested, and held to answer in the United States Court, on the same charge; the offered bail was refused, and he was lodged in jail. The case was subsequently tried before the District Court of the United States, at Milwaukee, on the question as to the right of a State judiciary to release prisoners, under a writ of *habeas corpus*, who may be in the lawful custody of United States officers; and also to determine the constitutionality of the Fugitive Slave Law. (*Washington Star*, September 20, 1854.) The Attorney General, Caleb Cushing, made himself very active in pushing forward this case. Mr. Booth, early in 1855, was fined one thousand dollars and sentenced to one month's imprisonment. John Ryecraft, for same offence, was sentenced in a fine of two hundred dollars and imprisonment for ten days. All for acts such as Christianity and Humanity enjoin. On a writ of *habeas corpus*, Messrs. Booth and Ryecraft were taken before the Wisconsin Supreme Court, sitting at Madison, and discharged from imprisonment. This, however, did not relieve them from the fines imposed by the United States Court. The owner of the slave brought a civil suit against Mr. Booth, claiming $1,000 damages for the loss of his slave. Judge Miller decided, July, 1855, that the $1,000 must be paid.

EDWARD DAVIS, *March*, 1854. As the steamboat Keystone State, Captain Hardie, from Savannah, was entering Delaware Bay, bound to Philadelphia, the men engaged in heaving the lead heard a voice from under the guards of the boat, calling for help. A rope was thrown, and a man caught it and was drawn into the boat in a greatly exhausted state. He had remained in that place from the time of leaving Savannah, the water frequently sweeping over him. Some bread in his pocket was saturated with salt water and dissolved to a pulp. The captain ordered the vessel to be put in to Newcastle, Delaware, where the fugitive, hardly able to stand, was taken on shore and put in jail, to await the orders of his owners, in Savannah. Davis claimed to be a free

2*

man, and a native of Philadelphia, and described many localities there. Before Judge Bradford, at Newcastle, Davis's freedom was fully proved, and he was discharged. He was again arrested and placed in jail, on the oath of Capt. Hardie that he believed him to be a fugitive slave and a fugitive from justice. After some weeks' delay, he was brought to trial before United States Commissioner Samuel Guthrie, who ordered him to be delivered up to his claimant, on the ground that he was legally a slave, though free-born. It appeared in evidence that Davis had formerly gone from Pennsylvania to reside in Maryland, contrary to the laws of that State, which forbid free colored persons from other States to come there to reside; and being unable to pay the fine imposed for this offence (!) by the Orphan's (!) Court of Hartford County, was committed to jail and sold as a slave for life, by Robert McGaw, Sheriff of the County, to Dr. John G. Archer, of Louisiana, from whom he was sold to B. M. Campbell, who sold him to William A. Dean, of Macon, Georgia, the present claimant. Thus a free-born citizen of Pennsylvania was consigned, *by law*, to slavery for life.

[☞ In May, 1854, the Kansas-Nebraska Bill was enacted, another triumph of Slavery, repealing the Missouri Compromise, and opening the whole vast Territory of the United States to slavery.]

ANTHONY BURNS, arrested in *Boston*, May 24, 1854, as the slave of Charles F. Suttle, of Alexandria, Virginia, who was present to claim him, accompanied by a witness from Richmond, Virginia, named William Brent. Burns was arrested on a warrant granted by United States Commissioner Edward Greeley Loring, taken to the Court House in Boston, ironed, and placed in an upper story room, under a strong guard. The hearing commenced the next morning before Mr. Loring, but was adjourned until Saturday, May 27th, to give the counsel for A. Burns time to examine the case. On Friday evening, (26th,) an attack was made upon the Court House by a body of men, with the evident design of rescuing Burns; a door was forced in, and one of the Marshal's special guard (named Batchelder) was killed; whether by the assailants or by one of his own party is uncertain, it being quite dark. Upon the cry of Batchelder that he was killed, the attacking party retreated, and made no further attempt. The trial of the case proceeded on Saturday, again on Monday, Tuesday, and Wednesday, when the Commissioner said he would give his decision on Friday. During the trial, Burns was continually surrounded by a numerous body-guard, (said to be at least one hundred and twenty-five men,) taken chiefly from the vilest sinks of scoundrelism, corruption and crime in the city, and made Deputy Marshals for the occasion, by Watson Freeman, United States Marshal. These men, with every form of loathsome impurity and hardened villainy stamped upon their faces, sat constantly round the prisoner while in the court-room, the handles of pistols and revolvers visibly protruding from their breast pockets. A company of United States troops, from the Navy Yard, occupied the Court House, and guarded all avenues to the United States court-room. The testimony of numerous highly respectable witnesses was adduced to show that Anthony Burns was in Boston a month earlier than the time at which he was said to have left Richmond. R. H. Dana, Jr., and Charles M. Ellis, counsel for Burns, made very eloquent and able arguments in his behalf. Seth J. Thomas and Edward G. Parker were the counsel for Suttle, the case being constantly watched and aided by the United States District Attorney, Benjamin F. Hallett, who was in regular telegraphic communication with the President of the United States, (F. Pierce,) at Washington. An effort was made, and followed up with much perseverance, to buy Burns's freedom, Suttle having offered to sell him for $1,200. The money was raised and tendered to Suttle, when difficulties were interposed, especially by Mr. Attorney Hallett, and the attempt failed. Suttle afterwards declared he would not sell Burns for any sum, but that he should go back to Virginia. On Friday morning, June 2d, Commissioner Loring gave his decision, overriding all the testimony in Burns's favor, using certain expressions which fell from Burns in the first heat and confusion of his arrest as testimony against him, and concluding with ordering him to be delivered up to the claimant. Some four hours were consumed in getting Court street, State street, &c., in a state of readiness for the removal of the prisoner.

A regiment of Massachusetts Infantry had been posted on Boston Common, under command of Col. Benjamin Franklin (!) Edmands, from an early hour of the day, in anticipation of the Commissioner's decision. These troops, which had been called out by the Mayor, Jerome V. C. Smith, were marched to the scene of the kidnapping, and so placed as to guard every street, lane, and other avenue leading to Court street, State street, &c., the route through which the slave procession was to pass. No individual was suffered to pass within these guards, and acts of violence were committed by them on several individuals. Court Square was occupied by two companies of United States troops, and a large field-piece was drawn into the centre. All preparations being made, Watson Freeman (United States Marshal) issued forth from the Court House with his prisoner, who walked with a firm step, surrounded by the body-guard of vile men before mentioned, with drawn United States sabres in their hands, and followed by United States troops with the aforesaid piece of artillery. Preceded by a company of Massachusetts mounted troops, under command of Col. Isaàc H. Wright, this infamous procession took its way down Court street, State street, and Commerce street, (for the proprietors of Long Wharf refused to allow them to march upon their premises, though a public highway in all ordinary cases,) to the T Wharf, where the prisoner was taken on board a steam tow-boat, and conveyed down the harbor to the United States Revenue Cutter Morris, in which he was transported to Virginia.

It may not be amiss to have given, in a single instance, this somewhat detailed account of the process of seizing, trying, and delivering up a man into slavery, whose only crime was that he had fled from a bondage "one hour of which is fraught with more misery than ages of that which our fathers rose in rebellion to throw off," as Thomas Jefferson, the Virginia slaveholder, himself declared.

Anthony Burns, having been sold into North Carolina was afterwards purchased with money subscribed in Boston and vicinity for the purpose, and returned to Boston, *free*.

The *illegality* of the Mayor's conduct in ordering out the military, and giving to the Colonel of the regiment the entire control of the same, was fully shown by different and highly competent writers, among whom was P. W. Chandler, Esq., whose two articles, in the *Boston Advertiser*, deserve to be remembered with respect. The Mayor's excuse was, that he desired to *keep the peace!* But these Massachusetts troops received pay for their day's work from the United States Government! Judge Hoar, in a charge to the Grand Jury, declared the act of the Mayor, in calling out the militia, to be an infraction of law. Men, assaulted and injured by the military force on that day, brought actions against the Mayor and the Colonel of the regiment, but obtained no redress.

STEPHEN PEMBROKE, and his two sons, *Robert* and *Jacob,* 19 and 17 years of age, were arrested in New York almost simultaneously with the seizure of Burns in Boston; claimed as the slaves of David Smith and Jacob H. Grove, of Sharpsburg, Washington County, Md. They escaped May 1st, and came to New York, followed closely by their masters, who discovered their retreat in Thompson street, and pounced upon them by night. At 8½ o'clock, next morning, they were taken before United States Commissioner G. W. Morton, "where the case came up for the most summary and hasty hearing that has ever characterized our judicial proceedings." Dunning and Smith were counsel for the masters, but the fugitives had no counsel; and the hearing was finished, and a warrant granted to the slave claimants, before the matter became known in the city. When Mr. Jay and Mr. Culver hastened to the court-room to offer their services to the prisoners, as counsel, they were assured by officers, *and by Commissioner Morton himself,* that the men wanted no counsel, and were not in the building. On search, however, it was found they were in the building, locked up in a room. They said they desired counsel, and the aid of friends. A writ of *habeas corpus* was obtained, but before it could be served, the three men had been removed from the State, and were on their way to Baltimore. [See the published card of E. D. CULVER, Esq.] Stephen Pembroke was the brother, and his sons the nephews, of Rev. Dr. Pennington, of New York city, Pastor of a Presbyterian (colored) Church. Stephen Pembroke was purchased and brought back to New York, ($1,000 having been contributed for that purpose,) and related his experience of the slave's life at a public meeting, held in the

Broadway Tabernacle, July 17, 1854. His sons had been sold, and remained in slavery.

Akron, Ohio. On Thursday of last week, says the Salem (Ohio) *Bugle*, a bold and outrageous attempt was made to kidnap a colored citizen of Akron. The kidnappers had been prowling about Cleveland for a week previous, but the colored people and their friends were on their guard, and they met with no success there. They next made a descent upon Akron, and visited a colored barber, named James Worthington, pretending a wish to buy his house. On a subsequent day, at 6 o'clock, A. M., they went to Worthington's house, and arrested him on a charge of *counterfeiting*, and took him to the railroad depot. W. begged his friends to get him counsel ; the alarm was given, and an immense crowd assembled. A paper, which the kidnappers produced as a writ, was examined, and found to be totally worthless. The excited crowd refused to let the man be taken away ; and the scoundrels were suffered to go away, alone. One of them was said to be from Louisville, Ky. ; another, a United States officer, from Cleveland. — *Bugle, May* 27, 1854.

Near Cedarville, Ohio, May 25, 1854, about noon, " a colored man, of middle age and respectable appearance, was walking on the Columbus and Xenia turnpike. He was alone. A man in a buggy overtook him, and invited him to ride, saying he was a friend to the colored man, and promising to assist him in obtaining his liberty." He took the colored man to the house of one Chapman, " three miles south of Selma, in Greene County." There Chapman and the other, (whose name was William McCord,) fell upon the colored man, struck him with a *colt* upon the head, so that he bled severely, and bound his hands behind him. " Soon after the negro got loose, and ran down the road ; McCord ran after him, crying : — ' Catch the d—d horse thief,' &c., Chapman and his son following ; negro picked up a stone, the man a club, and struck him on the head, so that he did not throw the stone. He was then tied, and helped by McCord and Chapman to walk to the buggy. McCord asked Chapman, the son, to accompany him to Cincinnati with the colored man, promising to give him half the reward ($200) if he would. They then started, driving very fast." " We had not gone over two or three miles," said Chapman, " before the negro died, and after taking him two or three miles further, put him out, and left him as now discovered : "—viz., in a thick wood, one mile south of Clifton. The above facts are taken from the testimony given at the coroner's inquest over the body. The jury gave in substance the following verdict : — "Deceased came to his death by blows from a colt and club in the hands of one William McCord, assisted by the two Chapmans." Chapman, the son, said that McCord made him a proposition to join and follow kidnapping for a business, stating that he knew where he could get four victims immediately. McCord was taken and lodged in Xenia jail. The Chapmans bound over to take their trial for kidnapping. — *Wilmington (Ohio) Herald of Freedom.*

JAMES COTES, free man of color, residing in Gibson County, Indiana, went to Jeffersonville, (Ind.,) to take the cars for Indianapolis. On going to the depot at 6, A. M., for the morning train, he was knocked down, "beat over the head with a brick-bat, and cut with a bowie-knife, until subdued. He was then tied, and in open daylight, in full view of our populace, borne off, bleeding like a hog." He was undoubtedly taken to the jail in Louisville. On crossing the river to Louisville, he met the captain of a steamboat, who knew him to be a free man. (About June 1, 1854.) The kidnapper was arrested and held to bail, in the sum of $1,000, to take his trial at next Circuit Court.

Columbus, Indiana. A Kentuckian endeavored to entice a little negro boy to go with him, and both were waiting to take the cars, when mischief was suspected, and a crowd of people proceeded to the depot, and made the kidnapper release his intended victim. *June*, 1854. — *Indiana Free Democrat.*

—— BROWN, a resident of Henderson, Ky., was arrested for aiding four female slaves to escape from Union County, Ky., to Canada. United States Marshal Ward and Sheriff Gavitt, of Indiana, made the arrest. He was lodged in Henderson jail. — *Evansville (Ind.) Journal, June* 2, 1854.

Several Kentucky planters, among them Archibald Dixon, raised $500, in order to secure Brown's conviction and sentence to penitentiary.

Nine slaves left their masters in Burlington, Boone County, Ky., on Sunday, June 11, 1854, having three horses with them. Arrived at the river, they turned the horses back, and taking a skiff, crossed at midnight to the Ohio shore. After travelling two or three miles, they hid during Monday in a clump of bushes. At night, they started northward again. A man, said to be a colored man, named John Gyser, met them, and promised to assist them. He took them to a stable, where they were to remain until night. He meanwhile went to Covington, Ky., learned that $1,000 reward was offered for their apprehension, and gave information of their place of concealment. At evening, a strong band of Kentuckians, with United States Deputy Marshal George Thayer, assisted by three Cincinnati officers, surrounded the stable, and took the nine prisoners, on a warrant issued by United States Commissioner Pendery. They were all handcuffed and taken to Cincinnati. Their names are thus given in the New York *Tribune* of June 20, 1854 :—Shadrack, aged 60 years, claimed by Jonas Crisler ; Susan, his wife, 29 years of age, and two boys, Wesley and John, 9 and 7 years of age ; Almeda, aged 26 years, and her child, Sarah Jane, aged 3 years ; Lewis, aged 24 years, all of whom, except Shadrack, were claimed by William Walton ; Lee, aged 21 years, husband of Almeda, claimed by John Gaines, as guardian of Elizabeth Ann and Jasper Blackenbecker ; Anderson, aged 22 years, claimed by John P. Scott. They were all given up to their claimants, and taken back to Kentucky.

A New Orleans correspondent of the New York Tribune, in a letter dated July 3, 1854, writes : — " During a recent trip up the river, I was on several steamers, and on every boat they had one or more runaway slaves, who had been caught, and were being taken in *irons* to their *masters*."

On the steamer Alvin Adams, at Madison, Ind., a man was arrested as a fugitive, and taken to Louisville, Ky. He was claimed as the slave of John H. Page, of Bowling Green. The Louisville *Journal*, edited by a Northern man, stigmatized him as a " rascal," for his attempt to be free. (July, 1854.)

Two colored men, on their way to Chicago, were seized and taken from the cars at Lasalle, Ill., by three men, who said they were not officers. The colored men were known to be free; one was "a respectable resident of Chicago." Some of the passengers interfered; but it being night, and very dark, and the cars starting on, the colored men were left in the hands of their kidnappers.

Chicago, Illinois. Three men from Missouri, with a warrant from the Governor of that State, to take a certain fugitive slave, seized a man whom they met in the street, bound him with a handkerchief, and to quicken his steps, beat him with the butt of a pistol. He succeeded in shaking off his captors and fled, a pistol bullet being sent after him, which did not hit him. He made good his escape. The men were arrested and held to trial, for assault with deadly weapons. By an extraordinary conspiracy on the part of District Attorney Hoyne, Sheriff Bradley, and others, these men were taken from jail to be carried to Springfield, Ill., two hundred miles distant, to appear before Chief Justice Treat, that he might inquire " whether said alleged kidnappers were justly held to bail and imprisoned." It was so suddenly done, that the counsel for the kidnapped man and for the State of Illinois had not time to reach Springfield before the men were discharged, and on their way to Missouri! The Grand Jury of the County (in which Chicago is) had found a true bill against them, of which the Sheriff professed to be ignorant, (which was deemed hardly possible,) — under which bill they would probably have been convicted, and sentenced to the State Prison. Thus the omnipotent Slave Power reaches forth its hand into our most Northern cities, and saves its minions from the punishment which their lawless acts have justly merited. — *Chicago Daily Tribune*, September 21, 1854.

☞ The three kidnappers published a statement in the St. Louis *Republican* of September 26.

☞ The case of SOLOMON NORTHUP, though not under the Fugitive Law, is so striking an illustration of the power which created that Law, and of the constant danger which impends over every colored citizen of the Northern States, fast threatening to include white citizens also, that it must not be passed over without mention. He was kidnapped in 1841, from the State of New York, and kept in slavery twelve years. Two men, named Merrill and Russell, were arrested and tried as his kidnappers, and the fact fully proven. But the case was got into the United States Courts, and the criminals went unpunished.

HENRY MASSEY, at Philadelphia, September, 1854, was brought before United States Commissioner, E. D. Ingraham, claimed by Franklin Bright, of Queen Anne's County, Md., as his slave. Arrested in Harrisburg.

HARVEY, arrested near Cumminsville, Ohio, — escaped, — taken again in Goshen, about ten miles from Cincinnati, and lodged in the jail of that city. An investigation of the case was had before United States Commissioner Pendery, and the slave remanded to the custody of his master. — *Cincinnati Commercial*, September 22, 1854.

Byberry, Pennsylvania, September 18, 1854. A carriage load of suspicious looking men came to this place in the afternoon. They waited until nightfall, when they burst into the house of a colored family, " seized the man in presence of his wife and another woman, threatening to shoot them if they interfered, — dragged him out, beating him over the head with a mace. The poor fellow continued to scream for help, until his voice was stifled by his groans; they forced him into their carriage and drove off, before any effectual assistance could be offered." He was a sober and industrious man, and much respected. His wife was left heart-broken, with one child. — *Norristown (Penn.) Olive Branch.*

The Frankfort (Ky.) Yeoman, of November 18, 1854, said : — " Kidnapping free negroes in Ohio, and deluding our slaves from their masters, to re-capture and sell them, is an established profession of a gang located upon the borders of the Ohio river, combining with negro-traders in the interior of this State." The names of some employed in this business are given, two of whom, having been arrested and imprisoned, threatened to burn the city of Frankfort for interrupting their business.

JANE MOORE, a free colored woman, at Cincinnati, November, 1854, seized in the house of her sister, (Sycamore street,) beaten, and with the help of a deputy marshal from Covington, Ky., carried over to Covington, and lodged in jail, on pretence of her being a fugitive slave. She was taken before the Mayor of Covington, " who heard the case with impartiality." Her freedom was established, and she released.

At Indianapolis, Indiana, December, 1854, Benjamin B. Waterhouse was indicted for harboring fugitive slaves, contrary to the provisions of the Fugitive Law. He was found guilty, but the jury recommended him " to the favorable consideration of the Court, and stated that the evidence was barely sufficient to convict." He was fined fifty dollars and to be imprisoned one hour, and the government to pay the costs. — *Chicago Tribune.*

A proposition for Kidnapping, on a large scale, was made by John H. Pope, "police officer and constable," in a letter dated " Frederick, Md., United States of America, January 1, 1855," and addressed to Mr. Hays, Sheriff of Montreal, Canada. " Vast numbers of slaves," says Mr. Pope, " escaping from their masters or owners, succeed in reaching your Provinces, and are, therefore, without the pale of the ' Fugitive Slave Law,' and can only be restored by cunning, together with skill. Large rewards are offered, and will be paid for their return, and could I find an efficient person to act with me, a great deal of money could be made, as I would equally divide. * * * The only apprehension we have in approaching too far into Canada is the fear of being arrested; and had I a good assistant in your city, who would induce the negroes to the frontier, I would be there to pay the cash. On your answer, I can furnish names and descriptions of negroes."
This letter was published, doubtless at the Montreal Sheriff's request, in the Montreal *Gazette,* January 13, 1855.
☞ The Montreal *Gazette,* of February 3, published a second letter from J. H. Pope.

A warrant was issued in Boston, January 10, 1855, by United States Commissioner Charles Levi Woodbury, for the arrest of JOHN JACKSON, as a fugitive from service and labor in Georgia. Mr. Jackson, who had been for some time in the city, was nowhere to be found.

ROSETTA ARMSTEAD, a colored girl, was taken by writ of *habeas corpus* before Judge Jamison, at Columbus, Ohio. Rosetta formerly belonged to Ex-President John Tyler, who *gave her* to his daughter, the wife of Rev. Henry M. Dennison, an Episcopal clergyman of Louisville, Ky. Mrs. D. having deceased, Rosetta was to be sent back to Virginia, in care of an infant child, both being placed in charge of a Dr. Miller, a friend of Mr. Dennison. Passing through Ohio, the above writ was obtained, by some Ohio citizens, who were informed of the circumstances. Rosetta expressed her desire to remain in freedom in Ohio. The case was removed to Cincinnati, and was delayed until Mr. Dennison could arrive from Louisville. (Ohio *State Journal*, March 12, 1855.) The girl was set free; " but was again arrested by the United States Marshal, upon the same warrant which Judge Parker had declared illegal; thereupon another *habeas corpus* was issued, which the Marshal refused to obey, when he was fined $50, and imprisoned for contempt." Even United States Commissioner Pendery, before whom the case was brought as that of a fugitive slave, pronounced the girl free, and she was placed in the care of a guardian. The United States Marshal being taken by *habeas corpus* before Judge McLean, of the United States Supreme Court, was set at liberty, Judge McL. alleging that the proceedings in the State Court were null and void ! A correspondent of the Ohio *Columbian*, writing from Dark County, Ohio, April 8, 1855, says :—

"While the 'right' of Rosetta was undergoing the forms of trial, in the Cincinnati courts, there were ten of the human species passed near that city, on their road to Canada. They consisted of two women and their five children, and two young men, and one boy, of 12 or 14 years of age. The mothers and their children were bright mulattoes ; one of the women was the daughter of a slaveholder, and so white was she, that any person, without a close inspection, would take her to be of pure Anglo-Saxon blood. On the question being asked what induced them to leave their Southern homes, they replied that their masters had a few months since sold to the South both their husbands, and as they had no friends or relatives left, they determined on the hazardous undertaking of escaping from a land of chains."

GEORGE CLARK, a colored boy, eighteen years of age, in Pennsylvania, was decoyed into the house of one Thompson, (February 23, 1855,) where he was seized by three men, one of whom was Solomon Snyders, a well-known ruffian and kidnapper in the neighborhood, who said to him, "Now, George, I am going to take you to your master." The screams of George fortunately brought deliverance to him. The three men were arrested, tried, and sentenced to imprisonment for kidnapping, by the Court of Dauphin County.—*Norristown (Penn.) Olive Branch.*

The Norristown (*Penn.*) *Olive Branch,* (in connection with the last-named case,) speaks of a case which had occurred a short time before, under the Fugitive Law, before United States Commissioner M'Allister, at Harrisburg, Penn., and which has not yet been mentioned in this record. A colored man and his wife, with their infant child, were taken, "one morning, very early," before Commissioner Richard M'Allister, and before any counsel could reach the spot, the case had been decided against the man and woman; but the babe, having been born in Pennsylvania, they did not " dare to send that " into slavery; " so the only alternative was to take it away from its mother," which was done, and that evening the man and woman were taken South. No time had been allowed to bring forward witnesses in their behalf, and there was only a single witness against them, and he a boy about seventeen years old, and a relative of the slave-claimant. The woman's sufferings, on account of the separation from her child, seemed greater than for her own fate. The article from the Norristown paper is in the *National Anti-Slavery Standard,* June 2, 1855.

GEORGE MITCHELL, a young colored man, at San Jose, California, arrested and taken before Justice Allen, April, 1855, "charged with owing service and labor to one Jesse C. Cooper, of Tennessee." Mitchell was brought into California by his then owner, in 1849, the year before the enactment of the Fugitive Slave Law. His arrest was made under a Fugitive Slave Law of California. By *habeas corpus* the case was carried before Judge C. P. Hester, of the District Court. Mitchell was discharged, on the ground (we believe) that the California Law was unconstitutional; also, that the proceedings were "absolutely void." On the 21st April (or May), "another attempt was made to reduce George to slavery, at San Francisco." He was brought before the United States District Court, Judge Hoffman presiding, claimed under the United States Fugitive Law as the property of the above-named Cooper. [The result of the trial not known.]— *San Jose Telegraph.*

At Dayville, Connecticut, June 13, 1855, an attempt was made to seize a fugitive slave; "but the citizens interfered, and the fugitive escaped." He was claimed by a resident of

Pomfret, who said he had bought him in Cuba.—*Hartford Religious Herald.*

At Burlington, Iowa, a colored man, called DICK, was arrested and taken before United States Commissioner Frazee. "Much excitement was caused." He was claimed as belonging to Thomas Ruthford, Clark County, Missouri. Dick was discharged as not being the man claimed. (June, 1855.)

A white girl, fourteen years of age, daughter of Mr. Samuel Godshall, of Downingtown, Chester County, Penn., while walking upon the road, was seized by two men, a plaster put upon her mouth, and she taken in a close carriage in the direction of Maryland. After going twelve miles, they put her out of the carriage, "in a secluded and woody portion of the country, threatening to kill her if she made any alarm, when they drove away as fast as they could." Some colored people met her, got the plaster off her mouth, and aided her home. It was supposed the kidnappers mistook her for a mulatto girl, but discovering their blunder, dismissed her.—*Philadelphia Ledger,* July 9, 1855.

The Norristown (Penn.) Herald relates a case similar to the preceding. Benjamin Johnson, a white lad of fifteen, on his way from his father's, at Evansburg, to S. Jarrett's, near Jeffersonville, was invited to ride by a man in a carriage. The man took him by an unusual route; night coming on, the boy was alarmed, and attempted to escape, "when the villain caught him and drove off at full speed, and by threats and blows prevented him from making any alarm." He drove to a distance of fifteen miles beyond Jeffersonville, when the boy succeeded in making his escape. (July, 1855.)

JANE JOHNSON, and her two sons, (colored,) brought into Philadelphia (on their way to New York and thence to Nicaragua) by John H. Wheeler. Stopped to dine at Bloodgood's Hotel. Jane there made known her desire to be free. Information of the same was conveyed to Passmore Williamson, Secretary of the Pennsylvania Abolition Society, an old association, founded by Benjamin Franklin, Benjamin Rush, and others. Mr. Williamson went to the hotel, and

found that the party had gone to the steamboat, at the foot of
Walnut street. He proceeded thither, found them, and told
the mother that she and her sons had been legally made
free by being brought by their master into a free State.
After some delay, Jane rose to leave the boat. Wheeler
endeavored to detain her. Williamson held Wheeler back,
and the woman went on shore, a number of colored persons
taking up the boys and carrying them from the boat. They
were enabled to escape. (July 18, 1855.)

The celebrated case of PASSMORE WILLIAMSON followed,
before Judge Kane, of the United States District Court.
(See "Case of Passmore Williamson," reported in full, and
published in Philadelphia, by Uriah Hunt & Son, 1856.) On
the 27th July, Mr. Williamson was committed to Moyamen-
sing Prison, by Judge Kane, "for a contempt of the Court
in refusing to answer to the writ of *habeas corpus*," — Mr.
W. *having answered* that he had not, and never had had, the
custody of the three alleged slaves, and therefore could not
produce them in Court. Mr. Williamson was kept in prison
until November 3d, when he was discharged by Judge Kane,
the technical "contempt" having been removed.

Five colored men, who were charged with assisting Jane
Johnson and children from the boat, were committed to
prison, excessive bail being demanded (viz., $6000 in one
instance, $7000 in two instances, and $9000 in the other
two) by Alderman James B. Freeman, who was afterwards
prosecuted by the said five men for corrupt and malicious
conduct in the case. See *Standard*, May 24, 1856.

CELESTE, a mulatto woman, claimed as a slave, before
Judge Burgoyne, Cincinnati, Ohio. It appeared that she
was brought to Cincinnati by her master, and she was set
free. — *Cincinnati Gazette*, July 7, 1855.

Two fugitives, in Indiana, (September, 1855,) requested
aid of the conductor of the Madison and Indianapolis Railroad. The aid given was to take them back to Madison,
whence they were conveyed over the river to Kentucky.
Before leaving that State, they had been hunted and attacked
by dogs. These they had despatched with their knives.
The conductor was dismissed from his position. An agent of

the express company was said to have aided him in the surrender of the men. — *Madison Courier.*

JACK, a colored boy, nine years of age, "claimed by
Joseph Tucker, of Mobile, as his slave, was sent back to his
master from Boston, in the brig Selma, Captain Rogers, on
the 18th inst." (October, 1855.) — *Boston Times.*

JACOB GREEN, a colored man, was seized near Hollidaysburg, Pennsylvania, by one Parsons, as a fugitive slave.
Parsons could show no authority for detaining Green, who,
with the help of some bystanders, released himself and
escaped. — *Hollidaysburg Standard*, October 24, 1855.

Four men indicted for kidnapping at Greensburg, Ind., in
the spring of 1855. Their names — David and Thomas
Maple, Morrison, and McCloskey. Charged with kidnapping
two men, whom they conveyed to a slave State, and sold as
slaves. The two Maples, fearing the indictment, absconded.
The other two were arrested, and brought to trial in October,
1855, at the State Court, before Judge Logan. "Defendants'
counsel moved to quash the indictment, for the reason that the
section of the statute of Indiana against kidnapping was in
violation of the acts of Congress, and, therefore, void; and
the Court accordingly quashed the indictment!" — *Indianapolis Journal.*

Eight fugitives from Kentucky reached Adams County,
Ohio, closely followed by several Kentuckians, who attempted
to search the houses of several of the citizens. "The people,
indignant at this outrage, assembled with arms, and placed an
injunction upon these summary proceedings." "The men-
hunters then offered $2,000 to any traitor who would betray
the fugitives into their hands. But, so far as we have learned,
the bribe was as unsuccessful as the attempted search." — (November, 1855.) — *Carroll Free Press.*

At Wilson's Corner, Bensalem, Bucks County, Penn.,
Dec. 13, 1855, a colored man in the employ of John Henderson was seized by three men, who tied him, threw him into a
wagon, and drove off at full speed. They were seen, and
quickly followed by men on horseback. After two hours'
hard riding, the kidnappers were overtaken. A fight ensued—
the black man was released; but three pistol shots were

fired by the kidnappers, killing a horse, and wounding one of the rescuing party severely. A statement of the facts was published, as an advertisement, in the Philadelphia *Ledger*, signed by William Williams and John Henderson.

" *Two very bright mulatto girls*," says the Staunton (Va.) *Spectator*, " one belonging to Mr. John Churchman, and the other to the estate of Colonel Crawford, deceased, took the cars at Staunton, on the morning of December 30, 1855, and made their way successfully to Baltimore, *en route* for a free State. At Baltimore, they were detected just as they were about to take the train for Philadelphia, and information of their arrest was immediately forwarded to D. Churchman, of this place." On the following Friday, they were taken back to Virginia. " They were so nearly white, that their success in imposing upon the conductors of the cars is not astonishing, and the only wonder is, that they were detected at all. Since their return, the girls have been sold — Mr. Churchman's for $1.050, and the other for $950."

FANNY, a colored child of five years old, was taken from Chicago, Ill., into Tennessee, and sold for $250. A man named F. M. Chapman, with his servant, William R. Tracy, were arrested as the kidnappers, and taken before Justice DeWolf. Chapman claimed to have owned the child in Arkansas, and to have brought her to Illinois [thereby making her free.] He procured Tracy to take the child to Tennessee, and sell her. The result of the case not known. (January, 1856.)

Two fugitives, passing through Ohio, (January, 1856,) were closely pursued and nearly overtaken, at Columbus, Ohio. "Ten minutes previous warning only, saved the fugitives from their pursuers." Deputy Marshal J. Underwood, being called on to act in the case, refused, and resigned his office, saying, he did not expect to be " called upon to help execute the odious Fugitive Slave Law." — *Cincinnati Commercial*.

☞ The following may, not improperly, find a place here. Where will the demands of slavery be stayed ?

The House of Delegates of Virginia, early in 1856, adopted the following : — " *Be it Resolved, by the General As-*

3

sembly, That our Representatives in Congress are requested, and our Senators be and are hereby instructed, to secure the passage of a law making full compensation to all owners whose slaves have, or may hereafter, escape into any of the non-slaveholding States of this Union, and there be withheld from those to whom such service or labor may be due."

MARGARET GARNER *and seven others*, at Cincinnati, Ohio, January, 1856. Of this peculiarly painful case, we give a somewhat detailed account, mainly taken from the Cincinnati papers of the day. It strikingly illustrates the manner in which, in nearly all instances, the laws and authority of the free States are swept away before those which the National Government enacts in behalf of slavery; and how little protection the poor and the oppressed can expect from either.

About ten o'clock on Sunday, 27th January, 1856, a party of eight slaves — two men, two women, and four children — belonging to Archibald K. Gaines and John Marshall, of Richwood Station, Boone County, Ky., about sixteen miles from Covington, escaped from their owners. Three of the party are father, mother, and son, whose names are Simon, Mary, and Simon, Jr.; the others are Margaret, wife of Simon, Jr., and her four children. The three first are the property of Marshall, and the others of Gaines.

They took a sleigh and two horses belonging to Mr. Marshall, and drove to the river bank, opposite Cincinnati, and crossed over to the city on the ice. They were missed a few hours after their flight, and Mr. Gaines, springing on a horse, followed in pursuit. On reaching the river shore, he learned that a resident had found the horses standing in the road. He then crossed over to the city, and after a few hours diligent inquiry, he learned that his slaves were in a house about a quarter of a mile below the Mill Creek Bridge, on the river road, occupied by a colored man, named Kite.

He proceeded to the office of United States Commissioner John L. Pendery, and procuring the necessary warrants, with United States Deputy Marshal Ellis, and a large body of assistants, went on Monday to the place where his fugitives were concealed. Arriving at the premises, word was sent to the fugitives to surrender.　A firm and decided negative was the response.　The officers, backed by a large crowd, then made a descent.　Breaking open the doors, they were assailed by the negroes with cudgels and pistols.　Several shots were fired, but only one took effect, so far as we could ascertain.　A bullet struck a man named John Patterson, one of the Marshal's deputies, tearing off a finger of his right hand, and dislocating several of his teeth.　No other of the officers were injured, the negroes being disarmed before they could reload their weapons.

On looking around, horrible was the sight which met the officers' eyes.　In one corner of the room was a nearly white child, bleeding to death.　Her throat was cut from ear to ear, and the blood was spouting out profusely, showing that the deed was but recently committed.　Scarcely was this fact noticed, when a scream issuing from an adjoining room drew their attention thither.　A glance into the apartment revealed a negro woman, holding in her hand a knife literally dripping with gore, over the heads of two little negro children, who were crouched to the floor, and uttering the cries whose agonized peals had first startled them.　Quickly the knife was wrested from the hand of the excited woman, and a more close investigation instituted　as to the condition of the infants.　They were discovered to be cut across the head and shoulders, but not very seriously injured, although the blood trickled down their backs and upon their clothes.

The woman avowed herself the mother of the children, and said that she had killed one, and would like to kill the three others, rather than see them again reduced to slavery!　By this time the crowd about the premises had become prodigious, and it was with no inconsiderable difficulty that the negroes were secured in carriages, and brought to the United States District Court-rooms, on Fourth Street.　The populace followed the vehicle closely, but evinced no active desire to effect a rescue.　Rumors of the story soon circulated all over the city.　Nor were they exaggerated, as is usually the case.　For once, reality surpassed the wildest thought of fiction.

The slaves, on reaching the Marshal's office, seated themselves around the stove with dejected countenances, and preserved a moody silence, answering all questions propounded to them in monosyllables, or refusing to answer at all.　Simon is apparently about fifty-five years of age, and Mary about fifty. The son of Mr. Marshall, who is here, in order, if possible, to recover the property of his father, says that they have always been faithful servants, and have frequently been on this side of the river. Simon, Jr., is a young man, about twenty-two years old, of a very lithe and active form, and rather a mild and pleasant countenance. Margaret is a dark mulatto, twenty-three years of age; her countenance is far from being vicious, and her senses, yesterday, appeared partially stupified from the exciting trials she had endured. After remaining about two hours at the Marshal's office, Commissioner Pendery announced that the slaves would be removed, in the custody of the United States Marshal, until nine o'clock Tuesday morning, when the case would come up for examination.

The slaves were then taken down to the street door, when a wild and exciting scene presented itself; the sidewalks and the middle of the street were thronged with people, and a couple of coaches were at the door, in order to convey the captives to the station-house. The slaves were guarded by a strong posse of officers, and as they made their appearance on the street, it was evident that there was a strong sympathy in their favor. When they were led to the carriage doors, there were loud cries of "Drive on!" "Don't take them!" The coachmen, either from alarm, or from a sympathetic feeling, put the whip to their horses, and drove rapidly off, leaving the officers with their fugitives on the sidewalk. They started on foot with their charge to the Hammond street station-house, where they secured their prisoners for the night.

The slaves claimed that they had been on this side of the river frequently, by consent of their masters.

About three o'clock, application was made to Judge Burgoyne for a writ of *habeas corpus*, to bring the slaves before him. This was put in the hands of an Ohio officer, Deputy Sheriff Buckingham, to serve, who, accompanied by several assistants, proceeded to Hammond street station-house, where the slaves were lodged. Mr. Bennett, Deputy United States Marshal, was unwilling to give them up to the State authorities, and a long time was spent parleying between the Marshal and the sheriff's officers. The sheriff being determined that the writ should be executed, Mr. Bennett went out to take counsel with his friends. Finally, through the advice of Mayor Faran, Mr. Bennett agreed to lodge the slaves in the jail, ready to be taken out at the order of Judge Burgoyne. Mr. Buckingham obtained the complete control of the slaves.

On the morning of the 29th, Sheriff Brashears, being advised by lawyers that Judge Burgoyne had no right to issue his writ for the slaves, and remembering Judge McLean's decision in the Rosetta case, made a return on the writ of *habeas corpus*, that the slaves were in the custody of the United States Marshal, and, therefore, without his jurisdiction. This returned the slaves to the custody of the Marshal. By agreement, the parties permitted the slaves to remain in the County jail during that day, with the understanding that their examination should commence the next morning, before Commissioner Pendery. Thus the State of Ohio was made the jailor of these slaves, while her officer, Sheriff Brashears, lyingly pretended they were not within the State's jurisdiction. An inquest had been held on the body of the child which was killed, and a verdict was found by the jury charging the death of the child upon the mother, who, it was said, would be held under the laws of Ohio, to answer the charge of murder. An examination took place on Wednesday, before the United States Commissioner. Time was allowed their counsel to obtain evidence to show that they had been brought into the State at former times by their masters. A meeting of citizens was held on Thursday evening, to express sympathy with the alleged fugitives.

The Cincinnati *Commercial*, of January 30, said : — " The mother is of an interesting appearance, a mulatto of considerable intelligence of manner, and with a good address. In reply to a gentleman who yesterday complimented her upon the looks of her little boy, she said, ' You should have seen my little girl that — that — [she did not like to say, was killed] — that died ; that was the bird.' "

The Cincinnati *Gazette*, of January 30, said : — " We learn that the mother of the dead child acknowledges that she killed it, and that her determination was to have killed all the children, and then destroy herself, rather than return to slavery. She and the others complain of cruel treatment on the part of their master, and allege that as the cause of their attempted escape."

The jury gave a verdict as follows:—"That said child was killed by its mother, Margaret Garner, with a butcher knife, with which she cut its throat."

Two of the jurors also find that the two men arrested as fugitives were accessories to the murder.

"The murdered child was almost white, and was a little girl of rare beauty."

The examination of witnesses was continued until Monday, February 4, when the Commissioner listened to the arguments of counsel, until February 7th. Messrs. Jolliffe and Gitchell appeared for the fugitives, and Colonel Chambers, of Cincinnati, and Mr. Finnell, of Covington, Ky., for the claimants of the slaves. A great number of assistants (amounting very nearly to five hundred) were employed by the United States Marshal, H. H. Robinson, from the first, making the expenses to the United States Government very large; for their twenty-eight days' service alone, at $2,00 per day, amounting to over $22,000. February 8th, the case was closed, so far as related to the three slaves of Mr. Marshall, but the decision was postponed. The examination in regard to MARGARET and her children was further continued. It was publicly stated that Commissioner Pendery had declared that he "would not send the woman back into slavery, while a charge or indictment for murder lay against her." Colonel Chambers, counsel for the slave claimants, in his argument, "read long extracts from a pamphlet entitled, 'A Northern Presbyter's Second Letter to Ministers of the Gospel of all Denominations, on Slavery, by Nathan Lord, of Dartmouth College,' he himself approving and recommending Dr. Lord's views." Colonel Chambers having alluded, in his remarks, to Mrs. Lucy Stone Blackwell, and said that she had sought to give a knife to Margaret Garner, the Court gave permission to Mrs. Blackwell to reply to Colonel C. Mrs. B. preferred not to speak at the bar, but addressed the crowded court-room directly after the adjournment. Her eloquent remarks will be found in the papers of the day. At the close of the hearing, February 14th, the Commissioner adjourned his court to the 21st, afterwards to the 26th, when, he said, he would give his decision.

Meantime, the case was making some progress in the State courts. Sheriff Brashears having made return to the Common Pleas Court, that the fugitives were in the custody of the

United States Marshal, Judge Carter said this could not be received as a true return, as they were in the County jail, under the sheriff's control. The sheriff then amended his return, so as to state that the prisoners were in his custody, as required in the writ, and this was received by the Court. The fugitives now came fully into the charge of the State authorities. The sheriff held them " by virtue of a *capias* issued on an indictment by the Grand Jury for murder."

The slaves declared they would go dancing to the gallows, rather than to be sent back into slavery.

On the 26th February, Commissioner Pendery gave his decision. First, he refused to discharge Margaret and three others from the custody of the United States Marshal, and deliver them to the Sheriff of Hamilton County, although held to answer, under the laws of Ohio, to the charge of murder. He then proceeded to consider the claim of Marshall to three of the slaves, decided it to be valid, and ordered them into Marshall's custody. He then considered Gaines's claim to Margaret and her three surviving children, decided that also to be good and valid, and ordered them to be delivered into the possession of said Gaines.

The case of the rightful custody, as between the United States Marshal and the Ohio Sheriff also came on, February 26th, before Judge Leavitt, of the United States District Court, and was argued by counsel on both sides. On the 28th, Judge Leavitt decided that the custody was with the United States Marshal. The substance of Judge L.'s argument and decision is found in the following extract: —

'Judge McLean says: — ' Neither this nor any other Court of the United States, nor Judge thereof, can issue a *habeas corpus* to bring up a prisoner who is in custody, under the sentence or execution of a State Court, for any other purpose than to be used as a witness. And it is immaterial whether the imprisonment be under *civil or criminal process.*' If it be true, as there asserted, that no Federal Court can interfere with the exercise of the proper jurisdiction of a State Court, either in a civil or criminal case, the converse of the proposition is equally true. And it results that a State Court cannot take from an officer of the United States, even on a criminal charge, the custody of a person in execution on a civil case.

" It is said in argument that if these persons cannot be held by the arrest of the Sheriff, under the State process, the rights and dignity of Ohio are invaded without the possibility of redress. I cannot concur in this view. The Constitution and laws of the United States provide for a reclamation of these persons, by a demand on the Executive of Kentucky. It is true, if now remanded to the claimant and taken back to Kentucky, as slaves, they cannot be said to have fled from justice in Ohio ; but it would clearly be a case within the spirit and intention of the Constitution and the Act of Congress, and I trust nothing would be hazarded by the prediction that upon demand properly made upon the Governor of Kentucky, he would order them to be surrendered to the authorities of Ohio, to answer to its violated law. I am sure it is not going too far to say, that if the strictness of the law did not require this, an appeal to comity would not be in vain."

Mr. Chambers said his client, Mr. Gaines, authorized him to say that he would hold the woman Margaret, who had killed her child, subject to the requisition of the Governor of Ohio, to answer for any crime she might have committed in Ohio.

Judge Leavitt's decision covered the cases of the four adult fugitives. Another legal process was going on, at the same time, before Judge Burgoyne, of the Probate Court, viz : — a hearing, under a writ of *habeas corpus* allowed by Judge Burgoyne, alleging the illegal detention, by the United St es Marshal, of the three negro children, Samuel, Thomas, and Silla Garner, which took place in the Probate Court, before Judge B., on the afternoon of February 27.

Mr. Jolliffe said he represented the infants at the request of their father and mother, who had solicited him to save the children, if possible.

Messrs. Headington and Ketchum appeared for the United States Marshal.

Judge Burgoyne said that, in view of the serious and important questions involved, he should require some time to render a decision. He intimated, however, that a majority of the Judges of the Supreme Court having passed on the constitutionality of the Fugitive Slave Law was no reason why he should not take up the Constitution and read it for himself, being sworn to support the Constitution of the United States and the Constitution of the State of Ohio.

Mr. Ketchum suggested that his Honor was as much bound in conscience to regard the decision of the majority of the Judges of the United States Courts as the express provisions of the Constitution itself.

Judge Burgoyne said, that however the decisions of the Judges of the United States Courts might aid him in coming to a conclusion, where the obligations of his conscience were involved, he could not screen himself behind a decision made by somebody else.

Judge Burgoyne subsequently decided that, in as far as the Fugitive Slave Law was intended to suspend the writ of *habeas corpus*—and he believed that it was so intended—it clearly transcended the limits prescribed by the Constitution, and is "utterly void." Judge B. required the United States Marshal to answer to the writ on the following Friday; and on his neglect to do so, fined and imprisoned him. Judge Leavitt, of the United States Court, soon released the Marshal from prison.

The *Cincinnati Columbian*, of February 29, gave the following account:—"The last act of the drama of the fugitives was yesterday performed by the rendition of the seven persons whose advent into the city, under the bloody auspices of murder, caused such a sensation in the community. After the decision of Judge Leavitt, Sheriff Brashears surrendered the four fugitives in his custody under a *capias* from an Ohio court, to United States Marshal Robinson. An omnibus was brought to the jail, and the fugitives were led into it—a crowd of spectators looking on.

"Margaret was in custody of Deputy-Marshal Brown. She appeared greatly depressed and dispirited. The little infant, Silla, was carried by Pic. Russell, the door-keeper of the United States Court, and was crying violently. Pollock, the reporter of the proceedings in the United States Court, conducted another of the fugitives, and all were safely lodged in the omnibus, which drove down to the Covington ferryboat; but, although a large crowd followed it, no hootings or other signs of excitement or disapprobation were shown.

"On arriving at the Kentucky shore, a large crowd was in attendance, which expressed its pleasure at the termination of the long proceedings in this city by triumphant shouts. The fugitives were escorted to the jail, where they were safely incarcerated, and the crowd moved off to the Magnolia Hotel, where several toasts were given and drank. The crowd outside were addressed from the balcony by H. H. Robinson, Esq., United States Marshal for the Southern District of Ohio, who declared that he had done his duty and no more, and that it was a pleasure to him to perform an act that added another link to the glorious chain that bound the Union. [What a *Union!* For what 'glorious' purposes !]

" Mr. Finnell, attorney for the claimants, said he never loved the Union so dearly as now. It was proved to be a substantial reality.

" Judge Flinn also addressed to the crowd one of his peculiar orations ; and was followed by Mr. Gaines, owner of Margaret and the children. After hearty cheering, the crowd dispersed.

" Further to signalize their triumph, the slaveholders set on the Covington mob to attack Mr. Babb, reporter for one of the Cincinnati papers, on the charge of being an Abolitionist, and that gentleman was knocked down, kicked, trampled on, and would undoubtedly have been murdered, but for the interference of some of the United States Deputy Marshals."

On the Sunday after the delivery of the slaves, they were visited in the Covington jail by Rev. P. C. Bassett, whose account of his interview, especially with Margaret, was published in the *American Baptist*, and may also be found in the *National Anti-Slavery Standard*, of March 15, 1850. Margaret confessed that she had killed the child. " I inquired," says Mr. Bassett, " if she were not excited almost to madness when she committed the act ? ' No,' she replied, ' I was as cool as I now am ; and would much rather kill them at once, and thus end their sufferings, than have them taken back to slavery, and be murdered by piecemeal.' She then told the story of her wrongs. She spoke of her days of unmitigated toil, of her nights of suffering, while the bitter tears coursed their way down her cheeks."

Governor Chase, of Ohio, made a requisition upon Governor Morehead, of Kentucky, for the surrender of Margaret Garner, charged with murder. The requisition was taken by Joseph Cooper, Esq., to Gov. Morehead, at Frankfort, on the 6th of March — an unpardonable delay. · Gov. Morehead issued an order for the surrender of Margaret. On taking it to Louisville, Mr. Cooper found that Margaret, with her infant child, and the rest of Mr. Gaines's slaves, had been sent down the river, in the steamboat Henry Lewis, to be sold in Arkansas. Thus it was that Gaines kept his pledged word that Margaret should be surrendered upon the requisition of the Governor of Ohio! On the passage down the Ohio, the steamboat, in which the slaves were embarked, came in collision with another boat, and so violently, that Margaret and her child, with many others, were thrown into the water. About twenty-five persons perished. A colored man seized Margaret and drew her back to the boat, but her babe was drowned! "The mother," says a correspondent of the Louisville *Courier*, " exhibited no other feeling than joy at the loss of her child." So closed another act of this terrible tragedy. The slaves were transferred to another boat, and taken to their destination. (See Mr. Cooper's letter to Gov. Chase, dated Columbus, March 11, 1856.) Almost immediately on the above tragic news, followed the tidings that Gaines had determined to bring Margaret back to Covington, Ky., and hold her subject to the requisition of the Governor of Ohio. Evidently he could not stand up under the infamy of his conduct. Margaret was brought back, and placed in Covington jail, to await a requisition. On Wednesday, Mr. Cox, the Prosecuting Attorney, received the necessary papers from Gov. Chase, and the next day (Thursday,) — again a culpable delay— two of the Sheriff's deputies went over to Covington for Margaret, but did not find her, as she had been taken away from the jail *the night before*. The jailor said he had given her up on Wednesday night, to a man who came there with a written order from her master, Gaines, but could not tell where she had been taken. The officers came back and made a return, ' not found.' "

The Cincinnati *Gazette* said : — " On Friday, our Sheriff received information which induced him to believe that she had been sent on the railroad to Lexington, thence *via* Frankfort to Louisville, there to be shipped off to the New Orleans slave market.

" He immediately telegraphed to the sheriff at Louisville (who holds the original warrant from Gov. Morehead, granted on the requisition of Gov. Chase) to arrest her there, and had a deputy in readiness to go down for her. But he has received no reply to his dispatch. As she was taken out on Wednesday night, there is reason to apprehend that she has already passed Louisville, and is now on her way to New Orleans.

" Why Mr. Gaines brought Margaret back at all, we cannot comprehend. If it was to vindicate his character, he was most unfortunate in the means he selected, for his duplicity has now placed this in a worse light than ever before, and kept before the public the miserable spectacle of his dishonor.

" We have learned now, by experience, what is that boasted comity of Kentucky, on which Judge Leavitt so earnestly advised Ohio to rely."

The assertion of the Louisville *Journal*, that Margaret was kept in Covington jail " ten days," and that the Ohio authorities had been notified of the same, is pronounced to be untrue in both particulars, by the Cincinnati *Gazette*, which paper also declares that prompt action was taken by the Governor of Ohio, and the Attorney and Sheriff of Hamilton County, as soon as the fact was known.

Here we must leave MARGARET, a noble woman indeed, whose heroic spirit and daring have won the willing, or extorted the unwilling, admiration of hundreds of thousands. Alas for her ! after so terrible a struggle, so bloody a sacrifice, so near to deliverance once, twice, and even a third time, to be, by the villainy and lying of her " respectable " white owner, again engulphed in the abyss of Slavery ! What her fate is to be, it is not hard to conjecture. But friendless, heart-stricken, robbed of her children, outraged as she has been, not wholly without friends,

> " Yea, three firm friends, more sure than day and night
> Herself, her Maker, and the angel Death."

At the risk of too far extending the record of this most painful yet instructive case, we give the following eloquent extract from a sermon delivered in Cleveland, Ohio, by Rev. H. BUSHNELL, from the following text : — " And it was so, that all that saw it, said, There was no such deed done nor seen from the day that the children of Israel came up out of the land of Egypt unto this day ; CONSIDER OF IT, TAKE ADVICE, AND SPEAK YOUR MINDS." — JUDGES 19 : 30.

" A few weeks ago, just at dawn of day, might be seen a company of strangers crossing the winter bridge over the Ohio River, from the State of Kentucky, into the great city of our own State, whose hundred church-spires point to heaven, telling the travellers that in this place the God of Abraham was worshipped, and that here Jesus the Messiah was known, and his religion of love taught and believed. And yet, no one asked them in, or offered them any hospitality, or sympathy, or assistance. After wandering from street to street, a poor laboring man gave them the shelter of his humble cabin, for they were strangers and in distress. Soon it was known abroad that this poor man had offered them the hospitalities of his home, and a rude and ferocious rabble soon gathered around his dwelling, demanding his guests. With loud clamor and horrid threatening they broke down his doors, and rushed upon the strangers. They were an old man and his wife, their daughter and her husband, with four children ; and they were of the tribe of slaves, fleeing from a bondage which was worse than death. There was now no escape — the tribes of Israel had banded against them. On the side of the oppressor there is power. And the young wife and mother, into whose very soul the iron had entered, hearing the cry of the master, 'Now we 'll have you all !' turning from the side of her husband and father, with whom she had stood to repel the foe, seized a knife, and with a single blow, nearly severed the head from the body of her darling daughter, and throwing its bloody corpse at his feet, exclaimed, 'Yes, you *shall* have us all ! take that !' and with another blow inflicted a ghastly wound upon the head of her beautiful son, repeating, 'Yes, you *shall* have us all — take that !' meanwhile calling upon her old mother to help her in the quick work of emancipation — for there were two more. But the pious old grandmother could not do it, and it was now too late — the rescuers had subdued and bound them. They were on their way back to the house of their bondage — a life more bitter than death ! On their way through that city of churches whose hundred spires told of Jesus and the good Father above ; on their way amid the throng of Christian men, whose noble sires had said and sung, 'Give me *liberty*, or give me *death !*'

"But they all tarried in the great Queen City of the West — in chains, and in a felon's cell. There our preacher visited them again and again. There he saw the old grandfather and his aged companion, whose weary pilgrimage of unrequited toil and tears was nearly at its end. And there stood the young father and the heroic wife 'Margaret.' Said the preacher, 'Margaret, why did you kill your child ?' 'It was my own,' she said ; ' given me of God, to do the best a mother could in its behalf. *I have done the best I could !* I would have done more and better for the rest ! I knew it was better for them to go home to God than back to slavery.' 'But why did you not trust in God — why not wait and hope?' 'I did wait, and then we dared to do, and fled in fear, but in hope ; hope fled — God did not appear to save — *I did the best I could !*'

"And who was this woman? A noble, womanly, amiable, *affectionate* mother. 'But was she not deranged?' Not at all — calm, intelligent, but resolute and determined. 'But was she not fiendish, or beside herself with passion?' No, she was most tender and affectionate, and all her passion was that of a *mother's fondest love.* I reasoned with her, said the preacher; tried to awaken a sense of guilt, and lead her to repentance and to Christ. But there was no remorse, no desire of pardon, no reception of Christ or his religion. To her it was a religion of *slavery*, more cruel than death. And where had she lived? where thus taught? Not down among the rice swamps of Georgia, or on the banks of Red River. No, but within sixteen miles of the Queen City of the West ! In a nominally Christian family — whose master was most liberal in support of the Gospel, and whose mistress was a communicant at the Lord's table, and a professed follower of Christ! Here, in this family, where slavery is found in its mildest form, she had been kept in ignorance of God's will and word, and learned to know that the mildest form of American slavery, at this day of Christian civilization and Democratic liberty, was worse than death itself! She had learned by an experience of many years, that it was so bad, she had rather take the life of her own dearest child, without the hope of heaven for herself, than that *it* should experience its unutterable agonies, which were to be found even in a Christian family! But here are her two little boys, of eight and ten years of age. Taking the eldest boy by the hand, the preacher said to him, kindly and gently, 'Come here, my boy; what is your name?' 'Tom, sir.' 'Yes, *Thomas*.' 'No sir, *Tom*.' 'Well, Tom, how old are you?' 'Three *months*.' 'And how old is your little brother?' 'Six *months*, sir!' 'And have you no other name but Tom?' 'No.' 'What is your father's name?' 'Have n't got any! 'Who made you, Tom?' 'Nobody!' 'Did you ever hear of God or Jesus Christ?' 'No, sir.' And this was slavery in its best estate. By and by the aged couple, and the young man and his wife, the remaining children, with the master, and the dead body of the little one, were escorted through the streets of the Queen City of the West by a *national guard of armed men*, back to the great and chivalrous State of old Kentucky, and away to the shambles of the South — back to a life-long servitude of hopeless despair. It was a long, sad, silent procession down to the banks of the Ohio; and as it passed, the death-knell of freedom tolled heavily. The sovereignty of Ohio trailed in the dust beneath the oppressor's foot, and the great confederacy of the tribes of modern Israel attended the funeral obsequies, and made ample provision for the necessary expenses! 'And it was so, that all that saw it, said, *There was no such deed done nor seen from the day that the children of Israel came up out of the land of Egypt unto this day;* CONSIDER OF IT, TAKE ADVICE, AND SPEAK YOUR MINDS."

Fourteen persons of color, held at Los Angelos, Cal., early in 1856, as the servants of one Robert Smith, were brought before Judge Benjamin Hays, on a writ of *habeas corpus*. Smith alleged that he formerly resided in Mississippi, where he owned these persons; was now about to remove to Texas, and designed to take these persons with him as his slaves. Judge Hays decided that they were all free, and those under twenty-one years of age were placed in the charge of the sheriff, as their special guardian. — *Los Angelos Star.*

The opinion of Judge Hays, (who is said to be a native of South Carolina,) is a very able one, and in the circumstances, of much interest. It may be found in the *Standard* of April 5, 1856.

Two colored lads, named RALLS and LOGAN, living in Cincinnati, were kidnapped thence by two men, named Orr and Simpkins, and taken to St. Louis, Mo., where the men tried to sell them. The men were arrested as kidnappers. (March, 1856.)

The Decatur (Illinois) Chronicle states that "a man charged with being a fugitive slave was recently arrested at that place, and carried off, no one knows where. The sheriff of the county was the willing instrument in the hands of the claimants; no attempt to appeal to the law was made, the negro being carried off as if he was a stray horse or dog." The Chicago *Tribune* says: — "If this is a true statement of the affair, that sheriff has laid himself liable to the charge of kidnapping, and should at once be proceeded against with such rigor as his offence demands." (April, 1856.)

☞ THE ASSAULT UPON SENATOR CHARLES SUMNER, in the United States Senate Chamber, by the South Carolina ruffians and Representatives, Preston S. Brooks and Lawrence M. Keitt, took place May 22, 1856.

Cincinnati, Ohio. Another Outrage. Last Sunday, as the steamer *Jacob Strader* rounded to the dock at Cincinnati, a free negro, who happened to be on board, was arrested by her officers, and immediately conveyed across the river to Covington. He exhibited to his captors papers which proved his freedom; but they paid no heed to his remonstrance. After lying in jail at Covington all night, he was taken out in the morning, and, after a careful hearing, discharged. What makes the matter worse, is the fact that the poor man got on board the boat at a town in Illinois, which was a proof that he was free. This outrage upon the dignity of our laws should be properly avenged. Let the captain and officers of the Strader be arrested on a charge of kidnapping; and, if they be found guilty, let them all be sent to the Penitentiary. There is no use in playing with such men. We apprehend, however, that the officers of justice in Cincinnati will pocket the insult to their State, and say nothing more about the matter. What are we coming to? — *Cleveland Leader*, May, 1856.

British Bark Intrinsic, Captain Macfarlane, on her voyage from Charleston, S. C., to Liverpool, had on board JOHN, "the property of Dr. Carrere," of Charleston. After being several days at sea, the captain discovered the fugitive, and, says the Charleston *Mercury*, "very correctly put his vessel about," and headed for Charleston. Falling in with the British schooner *Victory*, from Nassau, the fugitive JOHN was transferred to the latter, and taken to Charleston. — *Charleston Mercury*, June 10, 1856.

JAMES PECK, cook of steamer Ella, plying between Cincinnati and Nashville, together with the stewardess of the boat, were arrested for concealing and feeding a fugitive slave on board, and thrown into prison at Hawesville, Ky., to be taken back to Nashville. What their fate has been we have never learned; a long imprisonment at least, and, possibly, slavery for life, and the fugitive himself cast into a lower deep of the hell from which he had vainly essayed to escape. The stewardess was a mother, with' a babe of a few months old. — *Frederick Douglass's Paper*, June, 1856.

Boston, July, 1856. Bark Growler arrived in Boston harbor, from Mobile, having a fugitive slave on board. He was discovered, when four days out, — was then in a nearly starving condition, and much care was needed to restore him. He asked leave to go ashore at Boston, which the Captain refused, and undertook to confine him, with a view to returning him, as supposed, to Mobile. Whereupon the fugitive jumped overboard, and made for the shore; he was unable to contend with the current, and was picked up by a boat ordered out by the captain. These movements being noticed and understood on shore, a writ of *habeas corpus* was obtained, and the man forthwith taken before Judge Metcalf, of the Supreme Court. John A. Andrew, Esq., who acted as counsel for the prisoner, moved the Court that he be discharged. The Judge simply said, without note or comment, " Let Johnson be discharged; " which was immediately done, and he was soon beyond the reach of any designs upon his liberty. — *Correspondent of N. Y. Tribune.*

Some months later, the bark Growler again making a Southern trip, the owner of Johnson, says the Mobile *Tribune*, " Mr. R. Sheridan, pounced on her captain for the value of the slave, and got it—the owner's agent paying Mr. S. $1200."

" *A Grand Hunt for Negroes* came off in Greene County, Penn., the week before last, in which no less than fifty armed white men were engaged in the pursuit of nine negroes, who had left Booth's Creek, Harrison County, Va., a few days before. The fugitives — three men, and half-a-dozen boys, some of the latter but twelve or fifteen years old — escaped, and the " nigger-hunters " earned, not the reward of fifteen-hundred dollars they so anxiously sought, but the contempt of all honorable men. In one township, half-a-dozen of them drew their pistols on an unarmed woman, who refused to allow them to search her house for the runaways." — *Pittsburg Dispatch*, August 6, 1856.

Fauquier County, Virginia, summer of 1856. A Virginia paper says : — " A party of men from Frederick County arrested eight of a party of ten negroes, runaways from Fauquier County, near Bloomery, on the borders of Hampshire County. The negroes showed fight, were well armed with guns, &c. A desperate fellow drew his gun on Mr. Coohus, the muzzle nearly touching Mr. C.'sbreast; the gun missed fire, at the same time Mr. C. snapped a pistol at the negro ; the negro dropped his gun, drew a butcher's knife, and made at Mr. C., when another of Mr. C.'s party came up and knocked the fellow down with a stone, when he was secured. The other fellows were arrested after a show of resistance. Two of the party escaped. The negroes were lodged in jail at Romney."

Horrible Death of a Fugitive. A letter in *F. Douglass's Paper*, dated September 17,1856, ("names omitted for obvious reasons ") has the following : — " We had a fearful slave case here, a few days since, and which we dare not make public. A slave man was closely packed in a box at ——— ; the box was marked as goods, and consigned to a friend at this place, care of Adams & Co.'s Express. When the box was opened, the poor wretch was found dead, his countenance horribly contorted, and his body drawn into a knot. It appeared on examination that the box had no air-holes. Peace to his ashes ! ' O, Lord ! O, Lord ! how long ? O, that thou wouldst rend the heavens and come down ! O, let the sighings of the prisoner come before thee ! We are given up as sheep to the slaughter ! We are killed all day long ! O, Lord, avenge us of our adversaries ! ' "

Steamer Roanoke, on her trip from Norfolk, Va., to New York, October 5, 1856, brought the slave MOROCCO concealed in a box. He was discovered, however, before the vessel's arrival at New York, and was, by order of Capt. Skinner, conveyed on board a vessel bound for Richmond, Va., and taken back to Norfolk. The Norfolk *Herald* says : — " The boxing up of the negro was done in a house in Foster's Lane, not more than one hundred and fifty yards from the wharf of the New York steamers, and by two white men belonging to an Eastern schooner, who had the box conveyed on board the Roanoke ; and the inspector, whose duty it is to prevent the escape of negroes, was sitting on it, while keeping watch to prevent them from coming on board. Too much credit cannot be awarded to Captain Skinner and Purser Smith, of the Roanoke, for their prompt and judicious agency in securing the fugitive, and returning him to his owner." Hard as the case of the slave was, there is no doubt that Skinner and Smith were the chief slaves, and the basest, in the case.

Carlisle, Penn. The Loudon (Va.) *Mirror* says that the citizens of Carlisle, Penn., behaved very handsomely (!) a few days since, when a party of Virginians went to that place to capture some slaves who had run away. It says : — " When the fugitives were arrested and taken to the cars, an attempt was made by the free negroes and a few white men present to rescue them, but the United States Marshal was promptly in attendance, and took them into custody. The Mayor of Carlisle then addressed the crowd, and told them that the citizens of a sister State were there, in pursuance of law, to recover their property, and that they must not be molested. The great majority of the audience heartily seconded his remarks, and declared that they would sustain him. The slaves were removed by the officers without the slightest ·disturbance." — *Standard*, November 1, 1856.

New Albany, Indiana. Two fugitives were captured at Salem, Indiana, while stopping for breakfast at a public house. " It appears that they crossed the river on Sunday, and travelled on the railroad track all Sunday night. Having arrived within five miles of Salem, they gave a boy three dollars to take them to that place." Having asked for a private room, suspicion was awakened, and a man named Mc Kinney demanded their free papers—[free papers in Indiana !] The negro immediately drew a pistol and pointed it at McK.'s breast, but it missed fire. The bystanders then seized him, and his companion ran away, but was pursued and taken. They were both sent back to Louisville, Ky., whence they came.—*New Albany (Ind.) Ledger, Dec.* 3, 1856.

"*Jeffersonville, Indiana, Feb.* 7, 1857. If our city can boast of nothing more, she can at least boast of one of the most rapacious negro-catching Marshals that this State or any other can afford. Only a few days ago, he captured in this city, and lodged in the Louisville jail, a negro man— John Tatson—who asserts that he was born free in Virginia, where he was bound out until of age; after which he came to this State, where he has resided more than one year, as an upright working man, and as such is known to many of our citizens. He is now in jail, awaiting the clemency of the *Christian* laws of Kentucky, where, if he is not claimed by some pretended owner, or his friends in Virginia do not intercede for him, he will doubtless be sold into slavery."—*Correspondent of N. Y. Tribune.*

Kidnappers in Boston. "It was ascertained last evening that certain persons were in this city in pursuit of fugitive slaves. They applied to the wrong source for information, by which means the colored people were notified of the fact, and it was announced at the meetings of the colored churches, in order that they might place their brethren on their guard."—*Boston Telegraph,* April 9, 1857.

Slave-Catcher in Wisconsin. "A slave-catcher by the name of J——, of Virginia, has been prowling about this State after one of his escaped victims, a girl about eighteen years old. * * The chattel is on free soil, and the blood-hounds, official and volunteer, of this city can give him no help."—*Milwaukee Free Democrat,* April 21, 1857.

JOHN JOLLIFFE, Esq., an eminent lawyer of Cincinnati, "extensively known as the friend and advocate of the slave, in cases arising under the Fugitive Slave Law," (says the *Cincinnati Gazette* of June 1, 1857,) "on Saturday last was mobbed in Covington [a town in Kentucky directly opposite Cincinnati] and driven out of that town." Going over there to a friend's house, he was accosted in the street with profane and abusive epithets, by a man who gave his name as Gaines, the master and "owner" of Margaret Garner, in whose ever-

memorable case (given in preceding pages) Mr. Jolliffe had
nobly and indefatigably labored, as her counsel. Gaines
called Mr. Jolliffe "a d——d nigger thief," and collected a
mob around him. Gaines repeatedly assaulted Mr. J., and
very serious violence would have been done to him, had not Mr.
Warnock (an ex-United States Marshal) come up, took Mr.
J. by the arm, and guaranteed to see him safely to the boat.
Marshal Lett, having arrived, took the other arm, and they
walked towards the ferry, Gaines and the crowd following,
using every kind of threatening and insulting language. A
large man walking with Gaines cried out, "Get a cowhide and
cowhide him," and Gaines inquired at every house they
passed for a cowhide. He finally got a whip, and struck Mr.
Jolliffe with it over the shoulders, when Marshal Lett turned
and arrested Gaines. A German then came forward to assist
in protecting Mr. J., and he arrived safely at the ferry-boat.
Gaines was to be tried the next day. These facts are con-
densed from the *Cincinnati Gazette*.

ADDISON; *near Mechanicsburg, Ohio.* Addison was a fugitive slave from Kentucky, where he left a wife and children, free, but too poor to get to him; he had been living in
the neighborhood of Mechanicsburg, Champaign County,
about six months, working to get "enough to send for his
wife and children." A letter was written to his wife, which
was probably intercepted, and thus information of Addison's
whereabouts reached his master. On a Tuesday morning in
the latter part of May, 1857, a party composed of five Kentuckians and two Deputy U. S. Marshals, made a descent
upon the cabin of Mr. Hyde, where Addison resided. Addison took refuge in the loft of the cabin, through a hole barely
sufficient to admit his body, being a very large and stout man.
One of the Kentuckians mounted the ladder, with a double-
barreled gun in hand. He had scarcely got his head and
shoulders through the hole, when Addison fired upon him,
the ball striking the gun in front of the Kentuckian's breast,
and glancing off, whereby he narrowly escaped a fatal
wound. He immediately descended, fired his gun up the
hole, and retreated from the house. Meantime, quite a crowd
had been collected, and the party, alarmed, hastily left the
neighborhood. Addison took his immediate departure, and

was helped on his way by the Old School Covenanter Synod, who were holding a meeting at Northwood, in the adjoining county of Logan.

But the matter was not to end thus. The disappointed man-hunters returned to Cincinnati, and obtained a warrant from the United States District Judge, Humphrey H. Leavitt, for the arrest of four men, Hyde, Gurtridge, and two named Taylor, on the charge of aiding in the fugitive's escape; and on Wednesday, Deputy U. S. Marshal Churchill, from Cincinnati, arrested the parties above named in Champaign County, and started with them for Cincinnati. On application, a writ of *habeas corpus* was issued by Judge Baldwin, of the Probate Court of Champaign, for the relief of the prisoners, and put into the hands of the Sheriff, who made pursuit, and overtook them at Vienna, Clarke County. The Marshal and his *posse* refused to obey the writ, and there being a question of the Sheriff's right to enforce it out of his own County, the latter proceeded to Springfield, and put the warrant into the hands of Sheriff Layton, of Clarke County, who at once proceeded, with one assistant, named Compton, after the Marshal, and overtook him and his captives near South Charleston, where, without calling further aid, they attempted to arrest them. The Marshal and his company numbered some dozen men, and all made resistance; several shots were fired, none of which took effect, but the Marshal and his gang set upon Sheriff Layton, and beat him so badly that he was disabled, when they proceeded on. At Charleston, a warrant was got out against the Marshal and his *posse*, for assault upon Sheriff Layton, with intent to kill. This, with the writ of *habeas corpus*, was put into the hands of Sheriff Lewis, of Greene County, and he, with a respectable *posse* of selected men, started and overtook Marshal Churchill and party near Lamberton, and arrested them without difficulty; two of Churchill's gang, however, Bunker and Starr by name, effected their escape into the woods and got clear. The Sheriff took his prisoners to Xenia, and thence took the Marshal and *posse* to Charleston, to answer the charge of assaulting Sheriff Layton. The four men whom the Marshal had arrested were taken back to Urbana, in Champaign County, in obedience to the *habeas corpus*. These four men, while prisoners of the Marshal, Churchill, had been handcuffed and treated with all manner of indignity; and were threatened with having their brains instantly blown out if they opened their mouths to tell any body they were under arrest, or for what. "Such brutal conduct," said the Xenia *News*, "by United States officers, towards free white citizens of Ohio, deserves to be punished with the highest penalties of the law." Sheriff Layton was found to be badly hurt in the head and back, but not mortally; three or four of the Marshal's gang set on him at once, and one gave him repeated heavy blows with a colt. Sheriff Lewis had instructed his party, which consisted of some twenty resolute young men, thoroughly armed, that in case he (Lewis) was shot by Churchill, they were to fire at once. Churchill at first threatened to fire. Mr. Lewis told him if he did so, his whole party would be shot, when he submitted. His force, also, was well armed.

Churchill and party were examined and committed to jail in Springfield. They immediately telegraphed to U. S. Marshal Leifert, at Cincinnati, who in turn telegraphed to Washington for instructions. A writ of *habeas corpus* was issued by District Judge Leavitt, to bring Churchill and his men to Cincinnati, and Deputy Marshal Patton, with ten or twelve assistants, went to execute it. Meantime, Churchill and party were brought before Justice Christie, at Springfield, and arraigned on two charges,—one for assaulting Deputy Sheriff Compton, the other for assaulting Sheriff Layton, with intent to murder. Messrs. Churchill and Elliott asked, through their counsel, that the amount of bail might be fixed for their appearance at the next term of Common Pleas. Their bail was then fixed at $2,500 each, on both charges. The balance of the party, eight in number, were required to give bail in the sum of $10,000, and, refusing to do so, were all committed to jail. Two days after, Judge Leavitt's writ of *habeas corpus* arrived, when the Clarke County Sheriff gave up the prisoners, who were taken to Cincinnati for examination.

The above statement has been compiled chiefly from the Xenia *News* of May 29, 1857, the Cincinnati *Commercial* of May 30, and the Cincinnati *Gazette*. The course and language of the Cincinnati *Enquirer*, in this case, merits special reprobation. ·

On the 9th of June, the case of the United States Marshals, brought by Judge Leavitt's *habeas corpus* to Cincinnati, came on before the said Judge. George E. Pugh (U. S. Senator from Ohio) and C. L. Vallandigham (Representative in Congress) together with John O'Neil and Stanley Matthews, were counsel for the Marshals; for Sheriff Layton and the State, appeared Attorney General Wolcott, Rodney Mason, and James C. Good. The evidence showed a greater degree and amount of brutality and violence, on the part of the U. S. officials, than has been described in the foregoing account; the most of the Marshal's party drank frequently and deeply, and were much intoxicated. The evidence is too long for this tract, but may be found, taken from Cincinnati papers, in the National Anti Slavery *Standard* for June 20, 1857. The *Standard* says: —

"THE MAN-HUNT IN OHIO. We publish this week a synopsis of the testimony taken in the U. S. District Court at Cincinnati in the case of the Marshals, who ask that Court to release them from the custody of the State Judiciary. The evidence presents a picture of official ruffianism and brutality, at sight of which every American citizen may well hang his head for shame. The character of the American Government is fitly symbolized in the conduct of its agents. We shall see whether Judge Leavitt (an Elder in the Church and a member of the late Old School General Assembly) will extend judicial protection to these drunken scoundrels, or leave them to answer before the proper tribunal for their offences against the laws of the State of Ohio. We trust that Governor Chase will not fail in this case to vindicate the sovereignty of the State. The Columbus *State Journal* of the 6th inst. says: —

" ' We understand that Gov. Chase, at the earliest possible moment after reaching the city yesterday from Cincinnati, had an interview with Messrs. Mason & Good, who represent the Prosecuting Attorney of Clarke County in the case before the Federal Judge at Cincinnati, involving the right of the State to enforce her own criminal laws within her own jurisdiction, against violators, whether Federal, official, or other ; and that he immediately telegraphed to Attorney-General Wolcott to appear in the case on the part of the State, in conjunction with these gentlemen.

" ' In this prompt action we are certain that the Governor only fulfils the wishes of nine-tenths of the people of Ohio. Party discipline may restrain the expression of the real sentiments of the heart in some cases, but we do not believe there are many citizens of this State who desire to see her laws outraged, and her Sheriffs assaulted, beaten, and almost murdered, with impunity, by insolent Federal officials.' "

On the 9th of July, Judge Leavitt gave his decision, discharging all the Deputy Marshals from the custody of the Sheriff of Clarke County, declaring the Marshals to be right in resisting the State process, and that they had used no unnecessary violence ! SHAMEFUL !

A large meeting of citizens of Clarke County was held at South Charleston, wherein they fully supported the course of their Sheriff and the other officers, who arrested the U. S. Marshals — declared themselves ready to submit to any writ legally executed by *decent, sober* Marshals — denounced those partizan editors, who had misrepresented and slandered the citizens of Clarke County, " conspicuous among which editors for venom and meanness, is the editor of the Cincinnati *Enquirer*," &c.

On the 28th June, another descent was made on Mechanicsburg; in this case, by eight Deputy U. S. Marshals, with a view to arrest Messrs. Hyde and Charles Taylor, but they had both sufficient warning to enable them to escape the clutches of the hounds, who, being foiled, hurried away at early sunrise.

At various times, mostly early in July, the following persons, charged with obstructing the U. S. Marshals in the Mechanicsburg slave case, were all brought before United States Commissioner Newhall, at Cincinnati, and held to bail in the sum of $1,500 each, to appear and answer said charge at the October term of the United States Circuit Court, viz : Ichabod Corwin, A. L. Mann, Price Morris, residents of Mechanicsburg ; Samuel Lewis, Sheriff of Greene County, Sheriff John E. Layton, Deputy Sheriff James Fleming, Justice J. S. Christie, Attorney J. S. Hawk, Constable Alexander Temple, Deputy Sheriff William H. Compton, John C. Miller, and Constable E. Crossland, of Springfield. Thus was the sovereignty of Ohio ignominiously trailed in the dust before the power of slavery, incarnated in the Federal Government. And where was Governor Chase? And what use or meaning was there in having a State Government in Ohio?

At the assembling of the Court, Judge Leavitt instructed the Grand Jury as to what constitutes the violation of the Fugitive Slave Law. See *Standard*, November 21, 1857.

In April, 1858, nearly a year after the origin of the case, the prosecutions against the Ohio sheriffs and others were dismissed in the United States District Court, the District Attorney moving a *nolle prosequi*. And so Ohio was allowed to go out of Court, and went without the slightest remedy for all the violence and indignities which had been heaped upon her officers. It was said that the suits were discontinued by order of President Buchanan, Gov. Chase having advised that course, and saying the people of Ohio would not bear ...ir prosecution.

Another Slave-Hunt in Cincinnati. While the affair last described was yet remaining unsettled, the U. S. officers were summoned by one Col. C. A. Withers to arrest two of his slaves, Irwin and Angelina Broadus, (man and wife,) who had escaped from him in Kentucky. The following account of the matter is abridged from the Cincinnati *Commercial* and *Times*, of June 13 and 15, 1857 : —

" About ten o'clock Saturday morning, a bloody affair took place on Vine street, a few doors above Fourth. Deputy United States Marshal J. C. Elliott was severely stabbed by a runaway negro whom he was attempting to arrest, and the negro shot and desperately wounded by another of the United States Marshal's posse. It appears that two negroes, slaves of Colonel C. A. Withers, of Covington, Superintendent of the Covington and Lexington Railroad, had for some days been concealed in room No. 18 of the building adjoining the *Gazette* office on the north, which apartment was rented as a lodging-room by W. M. Connelly, reporter for the *Daily Commercial*. Friday night, the room was watched, and Saturday morning, warrants having been procured for the arrest of the fugitives, Deputy United States Marshals John B. Anderson, B. P. Churchill, J. C. Elliott, J. K. Lowe, James Woodward and E. B. Carty, proceeded to bag the game which had been treed. Woodward was stationed at the trap-door on the roof of the house, to prevent the possibility of escape in that direction. The others approached the room by the stairs. One of the party knocked for admittance. It was denied, when Elliott knocked out one of the panels of the door, when the negro man made a plunge at him with a dirk cane, inflicting a wound just below the third rib on the left breast.

" One of the party, said to be Withers, the owner of the slaves, then fired at the negro, the ball taking effect just below the breast bone. Elliott, as soon as he was stabbed, walked down the steps and across the street to the Custom-House, with a pistol in his hand. He was noticed by some bystanders, and assisted up the steps into one of the offices back of the District Court-room. The negro and his wife were al

4

brought over to the Custom-House, and placed in one of the rooms.

" Elliott received two wounds, one in the breast, near the left shoulder, the other in the left arm, near the elbow. The negro was shot in the abdomen. The instrument with which Mr. Elliott was wounded was a sword cane, the blade of which was bloody for eight inches. Dr. Blackman attended Mr. Elliott, and found that internal hemorrhage ensued from the breast wound.

" The captive negroes were taken at once before the United States Commissioner, E. R. Newhall, and in a remarkably short space of time were ascertained to his satisfaction to be fugitive slaves belonging to Col. Withers, and remanded to their master, to whom they were despatched in hot haste, the woman accompanying the Colonel in an omnibus, guarded by two Deputy United States Marshals, and the man being moved in an express wagon, with a guard of three of the Marshals. A warrant was issued for Connelly, in whose room the fugitives were found, but at the latest accounts, his whereabouts had not been discovered.

" We saw Marshal Elliott last evening. He was still in the office of the United States Marshal. He was *using an American flag for bed-clothing*, and evidently suffering much, dozing and moaning. At 9 o'clock last evening, Dr. Blackman reported him as improving, with prospects of recovery."

The wounded negro was taken from Covington to Cynthiana, Ky., where, after lingering a time, he died of his wounds. The ball, it was found, passed through his stomach, and entered his lung. " Freed at last," says the Ohio *Anti-Slavery Bugle*.

" *Nashville, Washington County, Illinois, July* 4, 1857. The citizens of this place have been engaged in celebrating the anniversary of Independence (! !) by holding an inquest on the dead body of a fugitive slave, shot last night in this vicinity. It appears that three runaway slaves from near Pilot Knob, Mo., were in the neighborhood, and last night a large crowd started out in search of them. After scouring the country for several hours in vain, the most of the crowd returned, but a detached party of six men encountered the fugitives, and ordered them to surrender. One of the negroes made fight, with a pistol in each hand, and was shot by one of the party named Mansfield, in self-defence. (!)   The negro died in an hour and a half.   The other two made their escape." An inquest was held on the dead body at Nashville, (which is in that part of Illinois called Egypt, on account of the prevalent ignorance and pro-slavery character of the population,) and on the day following "the grocery rabble carried the corpse out for burial, singing and drumming on the coffin the tune of 'Old Uncle Ned.'   Subsequently, a part of this same crew assisted the kidnapper to exhume the body, when the head was drawn across the corner of the coffin, and with an axe was dissevered from the corrupting remains, and being placed in a vessel of spirits, was taken to Missouri. * * * The honest German, from whose shop the axe was taken, was so horrified at the act, that he refused to receive the axe again upon his premises." (From the Chicago *Tribune*.)   "We can hardly believe," says the St. Louis *Republican*, "the latter part of the story.   It is too atrocious to be enacted by any man, unless in a moment of ungovernable passion.   One thing is certain, that it will find no justification — no palliation — among any considerable portion of our people " — with more to the same effect.   A horrible thing, it seems, to cut off a dead man's head for exhibition, but nothing calling for especial censure or remark to give chase to him with murderous weapons, and to shoot him dead — and all for the crime of loving liberty !   Nothing is said of the other two slaves, and we may hope, therefore, that they made good their escape. See *Standard*, July 18, August 1, and August 8, 1857.

Camp Point, Illinois, July 15, 1857.   A negro woman and three small children escaped from her master, living at La Grange, Mo., and came over into Illinois.   They hid in the woods several days, until hunger drove the mother to the vicinity of the house of James Welsh.   Meanwhile, it had been reported that a reward of $1,000 was offered for the apprehension of these fugitives.   A daughter of Welsh, seeing the mother and children, decoyed them to her father's house, by telling them she was a friend, and would give them food, &c.   "The distracted mother accepted this offer for her starving children, and, without suspicion, went to the house. Before they had time to appease their hunger, the sable mother, and poor, helpless children, were surrounded by a dozen stout men, *all armed ;* a hack was procured, and the poor creatures were soon fast returning to their bondage. — *Chicago Daily Tribune.*

Philadelphia, July 27, 1857.   A negro man, named JIM, who had accompanied his master, Charles Parlange, from New Orleans, left the said master for the purpose of tasting the sweets of freedom.   Mr. Parlange endeavored to secure the aid of the police, by representing that Jim had stolen two tin boxes, one of which contained money.   A telegraphic operator, named David Wunderly, was very officious in the case, saying that $100 (the reward offered) did not come along every day.   Probably JIM found friends, and his freedom was secured.

Springfield, Illinois.   Commissioner Corneau sent back into slavery an elderly negro, about sixty years of age.   He had been a slave in Kentucky ; in 1847 was sold by a Mr. Clemans, of Union County, in that State, to a neighbor named M'Elroy, with the express condition that he should be free at the expiration of seven years.   When this period had elapsed, M'Elroy agreed to pay him wages as a free man.   His wife and children have resided at Atlanta, in Illinois, free, for several years.   A few months since, the man came to visit his family, and staying longer than usual, M'Elroy sent a fellow named Markham with M'Elroy, Jr., after him, who arrested the old man while working in a harvest field.   A Democratic lawyer espoused the cause of the man-hunters, but objected to any counsel being allowed to the alleged slave !   This was overruled.   William H. Herndon, Esq., of Springfield, volunteered to act as the slave's counsel, and with assistance of Mr. J. E. Rosette, contested every inch of ground with ability and zeal.   But it availed nothing. — *Correspondent of Chicago Tribune,* August, 1857.

" *Cairo, Illinois, July* 27, 1857.   On Sunday morning, a party of Missourians, supposed to be nearly fifty in number, came over from the Missouri shore, to search for fugitive slaves — some ten or fifteen slaves having recently escaped from that part of the State.   They surrounded and searched several negro cabins, but at length the free negro residents, excited by their threats and insulting language, determined to permit no further search without a warrant, and offered determined resistance. A party of white men attacked u house near the Methodist Church. A number of shots were exchanged, and a Missourian, named Wilson, had his jaw blown off; the furniture of the house was entirely demolished, and about a dozen pistol-balls were left in it. The Mayor assembled a *posse*, and arrested three of the rioters, named J. Q. Stancil, Thomas Ewing, and — Gatilin. These were examined on Tuesday, before a Police magistrate, and were held to bail to answer a charge of kidnapping." — *Cincinnati Gazette, and other papers.*

It also appears that these men-hunters were very willing to diversify their sport by seizing occasionally free colored men. Two free negroes, about this time, had been forced across the river to be sold ; one of them escaped, swam the Mississippi, and returned naked to Cairo, beaten and mangled about the head.

"*Negro-Stealers in New Jersey.* On Monday evening last, three persons visited Belvidere, for the purpose of identifying certain negroes, (four in number,) resident in this neighborhood, who were suspected to have escaped from the *patriarchal* bondage of the South. Finding their papers to be defective and informal, they were compelled to return on Tuesday morning for further vouchers. In the meantime, the suspected fugitives got wind of the danger, and fled to a place of safety. Among these fugitives from home and friends was an old and respected negro, who has resided in Belvidere for thirty-seven years, gathering around him a family, and acquiring considerable property, and being a worthy and respected member of the Methodist Church in this place. These cases were ferreted out by one John M. Bryan, residing in Belvidere, who conferred with the masters, living in Delaware, and thus sold himself to this nefarious business, for about as many pieces of silver as Judas received for the betrayal of his Master." — *Belvidere (N. J.) Intelligencer ;* in *Standard,* August 22, 1857.

Wheeling, Virginia. " Two black girls, owned by Hugh Nichols, of Wheeling, succeeded in escaping to the Ohio side of the river. Immediate pursuit was made, the girls were

overtaken between Bridgeport and Martinsville, and carried
back to slavery."

"*Appeal to the Benevolent.* Mr. William Cockerel, an
American slave, who was whipped, imprisoned, hunted and
caught by bloodhounds, shot, robbed of wife, children, education, wages, every thing, — and who, after his escape from
Southern bondage, was twice arrested in Illinois, incarcerated
in a felon's prison, sold out at auction, in pursuance of Illinois
law, and at last made his final escape to Canada, is in this
city, for the purpose of obtaining the means of redeeming his
only son from bondage. His case appeals strongly to the benevolent." — *Boston Traveller ;* in *Standard*, September
19, 1857.

A young white woman, who came from Kansas with a man
named Halliburton, was sold by him as a slave, in Carrolton,
La., to a trader named White. She fled from his domicil,
and sought protection in a neighboring parish. She represented that she was an orphan, and left in charge of a guardian,
who went to California ; that Halliburton informed her that
he had received a letter from her guardian, requesting him to
take the girl to New Orleans, and send her on to him in California. The case is surrounded by mystery. — *New Orleans
Correspondent of the St. Louis Leader.*

[Though not strictly a case under the Fugitive Slave Law,
this is inserted as one of a great number recorded in the jour-
nals of both men and women turning kidnappers of children
and others ; the occurrence of which may be in a great
measure ascribed to that law, and to the mercenary, lustful
and diabolical spirit it nurtures.]

A Methodist Church fleeing to a City of Refuge. Under
this head the New York *Independent* details a case of a very
touching character, which it has responsible authority for
saying may be relied upon in all its facts. It is too instructive to be withheld, and does not admit of abridgement : —

" A few days since, I was travelling in the neighborhood of the great
road, (once governmental, when it was constitutional for the General Government to have roads or build them,) leading from the capital of the
Union to the '*frontiers.*' Here I saw what the historic page describes, but
which I hoped my eyes and heart would never be pained with seeing — a

church fleeing for refuge. Some on foot, leading their children by the hand, others in wagons, and following the 'leading of the better Providence,' were forsaking their homes, lands, neighbors, and the church of their adoption, to find, under the flag of the Crown, that 'liberty and the pursuit of happiness' denied them under the *stars and stripes*.

"Tears and sorrows were their companions. Yet, hidden by their heaving bosoms were hearts strong in the faith of the covenant-keeping God, that under a colder sky, and on a more congenial soil, His blessed manifestations they should enjoy, and their blood, and the blood of their kindred and children, no man should dare to claim. True, they had left farms and firesides, homes and friends, but they were carrying with them the altar in the heart, and the Shekinah.

"As I wished them a hearty God speed, I remembered that at the last quarterly meeting of the Methodist Episcopal Church, I had seen them surround the altar, and there commune, with myself and others, at the table of the Lord. I thought, as I ran over the names of the remnant left, and behold, here was a large moiety of the Church — enough to form a new church, 'fleeing into the wilderness.' I thought, too, of Pastor Robinson's church, in the Mayflower — that Puritan church, from the West of England, among whom were my maternal ancestors; of that church which fled to Holland, numbering with it my paternal ancestors; of the Huguenots, who found in the Georgians that freedom to worship God which France denied. A host of worthy examples came crowding into my mind; the Holy Family, too, who had sought and obtained in Egypt, liberty and life, that the constituted authorities of the Fatherland had refused them; and I said to myself, they are in good company. Better to cast in my lot with these, than with the Herods, and Henrys, and Harleses, and other oppressors of God's people.

"The pursuer was on their track; they were the hunted, panting fugitives. So, too, the minions of Herod sought for my infant Lord. I could not be ashamed of them. Before them were the wilds of Canada, and hardships, poverty, and suffering. But Liberty, blessed spirit, was there also. Behind them was the hated rice-field and cotton, and slavery.

"I knew where they were from, and who claimed them, and my duties under the Constitution, in the mind of their claimant; but I remembered *who owned* them, having *purchased them* with *His own blood;* and no Marshal's baton, no power on earth, should have persuaded or forced me to detain them a moment. Let no man talk to me of *law,* and my duties as a *law-abiding* subject. I am a law-abiding and *law-loving* subject, as were all my fathers before me; but my mothers have been scourged, fined, imprisoned, for refusing to obey the laws of the crown of England — *self-constituted authorities of God* — and their descendant honors and venerates them for their disobedience. Their blood flows freely and hotly in his veins. It curdles at the Fugitive Slave Law, and will spill the last drop, before yielding the slightest obedience to it. Law must commend itself to my *conscience,* before I can *conscientiously obey* it. My conscience is not the creature of the law, but above it, beyond it, could exist without it. A violated conscience, what law can heal? Yet I would not resist *by force* this law, however hateful or odious, nor would I resist any law. It is one thing to resist, and another thing to refuse to obey. A refusal to obey may call for penalties, and stripes may be gloried in, and a dungeon become the paradise of God. R. P. S."

See also Salem (Ohio) *Anti-Slavery Bugle*, September 20, 1857.

Cincinnati, Ohio. Two Cincinnati officers discovered at the river side a number of men endeavoring to force a negro man, whom they accused of having stolen a carpet-bag, across the river to the Kentucky side. The officers took the negro into custody, and placed him in a station-house; but after keeping him there awhile, and no one appearing to claim him, he was discharged. The negro said he had been a slave, but was liberated by his master in Cincinnati, who had then unexpectedly returned and claimed ownership, and had forced him to the river, when the officers took him in charge. — *Cincinnati Commercial*, September 28, 1857.

Washington, October, 1857. MATILDA SMITH, the slave of a Mr. Martin, of Maryland, had been manumitted by the latter in the summer of 1856, on receiving the sum of $75 from Mr. Lewis Clephane, a well-known anti-slavery gentleman of Washington; it being then supposed that the said Matilda was in or near Boston. She was an elderly person, and blind of one eye. About Christmas, 1856, Matilda appeared in Washington, which fact becoming known to her former master, Martin, he caused her to be arrested as a fugitive slave and brought before a magistrate, alleging that she had never been in Boston at all, but had been concealed in Washington. His deed of manumission being produced, he declared it to be worthless, as the woman had never belonged to him, but to his wife, and that he had no right to sell her! Case postponed a few days. — *Corr. of N. Y. Tribune,* Oct. 20, 1857.

BEN (*or* BENJAMIN CHELSOM), a slave near Lexington, Ky., was emancipated in 1840, by will of his master, and went to Ohio to live. The heirs of his master were unwilling to lose so valuable a piece of property, and tried various schemes to get possession of him. At length, they employed a negro man to decoy him to a place on the shore of the Ohio River; and there his kidnappers were lying in wait for him. They pounced upon Ben, who "fought with the desperation of a man who had tasted the sweets of liberty, after having spent half a life in slavery, and it was not until he had been several times brought to the ground with a stick, and his head severely cut and bruised, that he yielded to his captors, who bound him, and took him to Covington jail, whence he was sent to A. M. Robinson, Estil County, Kentucky." — *Cincinnati Gazette*, Oct. 26 and 27, 1857.

Newtown, Somerset Co., New Jersey. A colored boy named HENRY EDWARDS, kidnapped by two men, and carried rapidly away in a wagon, arriving at Bordentown at 4, A. M. Here the boy contrived, by kicking against the side of the wagon, to call attention, when two of the bridge men came and discovered him, bound and gagged. They took him from the wagon, when his kidnappers applied the whip to the horse and drove off at full speed. The boy, on being freed, started for home on foot, which he reached on Saturday evening, having been carried off on Wednesday evening. — *New York Tribune;* in *Standard*, Nov. 14, 1857.

Cincinnati, Ohio. Three slaves, brought by their master, a Mr. Withers of Virginia, stopped at the Cincinnati landing on their way to St. Louis; while the boat lay there, the slaves were taken by a writ of *habeas corpus*, granted by Judge Burgoyne of the Probate Court, and brought before Judge B. on a Monday afternoon. By request of counsel, the examination was continued to the next day, and the slaves meantime committed to the care of Mr. Eggleston, as guardian, according to an Ohio law. But on Tuesday morning, Withers obtained another writ of *habeas corpus*, from Judge Carter, of the Common Pleas Court, alleging his slaves to be illegally detained. They were brought before Judge Carter, when the following conversation occurred : *Judge C.* "Are you a slave?" *Ans.* "I am." *Judge C.* "Do you wish to go with your master?" *Ans.* "I do." *Judge C.* "You are at liberty to go where you please." The same questions were put to the others, with like answers; when Judge C. directed the Sheriff to hand over the slaves to the custody of Mr. Withers, and they were immediately rushed out of the court-room, put into an express-wagon waiting at the door, and driven with speed to the Vine Street Ferry, put on board the steamer *Queen City*, and in a few minutes were landed on the Kentucky side.

The sly, under-handed way in which the re-delivery of the slaves was made at the Court-House probably prevented a scene of excitement. An attempt was made, by Mr. Jolliffe, to obtain from Judge Burgoyne a writ against Alfred George

4

Washington Carter (the Judge), for a contempt of Court. Judge Burgoyne declined this, on account of the clashing of jurisdiction, although he said he felt bound to protect the process of his Court.   He ordered an attachment upon the slaves to be issued at once.   Judge Burgoyne further stated, that Judge Carter had said he should take *no further action in the matter* until the proceeding in the Probate Court was disposed of! — *Boston Journal ;* in *Standard*, Nov. 21, 1857.

Judge Burgoyne caused proceedings to be instituted against the lawyer, J. J. Dennis, who sued out the second writ of *habeas corpus*, while the first was still undisposed of. Mr. Dennis was brought before Judge Burgoyne, and it was shown that he had procured an adjournment of the Court of Common Pleas, under pretence of preparing for trial as counsel for Million, claimant of other slaves, and then, with Judge Carter as an accomplice, smuggling eight human beings into Kentucky slavery.   The Ohio *Bugle* says:— " Judge Burgoyne has in this and in the Margaret Garner case, shown more manhood and self-respect than any other representative of the vaunted sovereignty of Ohio, and has alone attempted to maintain the dignity and authority of his Court.   For such an intolerable offence against the peace and dignity of slaveholding rule, he is now to be pursued with prosecutions and vexatious suits, got up by kidnappers and their abetting attorneys and judges.   This process has been commenced, as we learn by the following paragraph from the Cincinnati *Gazette* of Monday last :

" The recent proceedings in the case of alleged contempt of the Probate Court, growing out of the return of the eight slaves to Kentucky, has given rise to a prosecution in another shape.   Yesterday afternoon, about 4 o'clock, Constable McLaughlin arrested Judge Burgoyne on a warrant issued by J. J. McFall, Esq., and took him before that officer, to answer a charge of oppression in office.

" The affidavit upon which the warrant was granted was made by J. J. Dennis, Esq.   The particular ground of complaint we understand to be the infliction of the fine of $500 upon that gentleman, for the alleged contempt of the Probate Court, the refusal to permit Mr. D. to say any thing in his own defence at the time the sentence was passed, and various acts of oppression connected with the hearing of the case.

"Judge Burgoyne was taken before Justice McFall, who held him in bonds of $1,000 for his appearance for examination." — *Bugle*, Dec. 12, 1857.

DAVID WAIT, of Adams County, Ohio, indicted for aiding, abetting, and harboring fugitive slaves, was brought for trial before the United States Court in Cincinnati; Judge Leavitt presiding. In this trial, Mr. B. Million, of Kentucky, the alleged owner of the slaves, (eight in number,) and the principal witness against Wait, gave testimony so contradictory to what he had avowed to several persons previously, that he was immediately put on trial for perjury. It was proved by credible witnesses that he had declared that the negroes had crossed the river with his consent, in order to get them beyond the reach of his creditors. Judge Leavitt, in charging the jury, said that, if the slaves left Kentucky by consent of their master, the verdict should be in their (the slaves') favor. The jury were out one day and night, could not agree, and were discharged. It was underderstood they were nine for conviction, and but three for acquittal!

JAMES PUNTNEY, also, was arrested on complaint of said Million for harboring his eight slaves, and was held to bail in $500 to answer to the charge. B. Million, being brought before Commissioner Lee, on the charge of perjury, was discharged! — *Cincinnati Gazette;* and *Standard*, of Nov. 21 and 28, 1857.

Geneva (N. Y.) Kidnapping Case. This case is so illustrative of the spirit engendered by the Fugitive Slave Law, as to demand notice in a publication like this:

Two young colored men, or lads, 18 or 20 years of age, residing in Geneva, New York, were induced, by the promise of liberal wages, to leave that place for Columbus, Ohio, to work in a hotel there. Their names were Daniel Prue and John F. Hite. The man who offered them the wages, and who was to accompany them to Columbus, was Napoleon B. Van Tuyl, only some 21 years of age, a clerk in a dry goods store at Geneva, and son of a respectable citizen of Penn Yan, N. Y. He was, says the *Yates County Chronicle*, "the only remaining child of his parents, and had hitherto maintained an honest character; he was also a *professor of religion and a member of a religious church.*" [The distinction between a *religious* and a *Christian* church is suggested by these words, — a distinction exceedingly important to be borne in mind.] We copy now from the *Cincinnati Gazette*, of several dates from 3d of December, 1857, onward:

The history in brief is thus : On the cars from Cleveland, Van Tuyl, the kidnapper of the negroes, fell in company with three Kentuckians, Barton W. Jenkins, of Port Royal, Henry County, and Henry Giltner and George W. Metcalf, of Carroll County, to whom he represented the boys as runaway slaves, and solicited their aid in getting them back to Tennessee, from which State Van Tuyl asserted they had escaped. The three gentlemen named, placing implicit reliance in the story of the kidnapper, who gave his name as Paul Lensington, rendered him such assistance as was in their power, and when the boy Daniel Prue, who, it seems, had overheard a part of the false tale of Van Tuyl, and who had also learned that the cars had passed Columbus, where he expected to stop, attempted to get off the cars at Carlisle, Mr. Jenkins made an effort to keep him on, which Prue resisted and knocked him down, and escaped and went back to Columbus on foot. Jenkins subsequently went back with Van Tuyl in search of him, and was afterwards arrested at Franklin on charge of kidnapping, but discharged for want of evidence.

The other boy (John Hite) remained on board the cars, still believing that the men were acting in good faith, and that every thing would be satisfactory. He was brought to this city, (Cincinnati,) conveyed across the river to Covington, and from there shipped down the river and placed in jail at Carrolton, Ky.

Certified copies of the freedom papers of Hite were forwarded to Judge Wilcox, of Columbus, together with a letter from Hon. Sam'l F. Vinton, giving a full description of him. He had been a servant in Mr. Vinton's family in Washington, where his father now lives. The free papers and Mr. Vinton's letter were given to Judge Calvin Walker, who went to Kentucky, by authority of the Governor of New York, to ferret out the matter, accompanied by Mr. Robert Lay, of Geneva, for whom Hite had formerly worked, and who could therefore readily identify him.

But to return to the order of the narrative:

Van Tuyl (or Lensington, as he was known to the Kentuckians) came to Kentucky a day or two after, and made a sale of the boy to Jenkins for $500, alleging, in the bill which has been shown us [Editors of *Gazette*], that he was "19 years of age, of copper color; that he was the true and lawful owner of said boy, and that he was a slave for life," which he signed "Paul Lensington." The bill of sale was made out for $750, but $500 only was paid, the balance being voluntarily deducted by Van Tuyl for the trouble of the purchaser in aiding him to secure his "property." Subsequently, the negro was sold to Lorenzo Graves, Esq., by Mr. Jenkins, for $750, who took him to Warsaw, Ky., but afterwards sent him to Louisville, to be confined until he should require his services elsewhere. This brings the history of the case down to the arrival of Mr. Walker with the requisition from the Governor of New York.

On the arrival of the two New York officers at Warsaw, they had no difficulty in finding Mr. Graves, and on explaining to him their business, and exhibiting the evidence in their possession that the negro was free, that gentleman replied, "I am satisfied he is a free negro, and that he has been kidnapped. I am a Kentuckian and a slaveholder, but I would as soon poison my mother as to purchase a negro I knew to be free. I pledge you my honor that the boy shall be placed in your hands, and safely conveyed to a free State." Like an honorable man, he kept his word in every particular.

Mr. Graves immediately had horses saddled for the party, and proceeded to the residence of Mr. Jenkins, who had made the sale to Mr. Graves, and that gentleman was as much astonished as had been Mr. Graves, that he had been so foully imposed upon by the rascal Van Tuyl, and immediately refunded to Mr. Graves the amount of the purchase money, putting to his private loss account the $500 paid to Van Tuyl, merely reminding the officers, if any portion of the amount could be obtained from "Mr. Lensington," that it should be forwarded. Matters being satisfactorily arranged thus far, the whole party started for Louisville, where Hite was still in confinement, and Mr. Graves not only opened the prison doors of the captive, with his own hands, and delivered him to Mr. Walker, but he accompanied the gentlemen with the boy to this city, gave the latter money to spend on the way, and on his arrival here, bought several acceptable presents to send to the boy's mother at Geneva. In reply to Mr. Walker, as he was about leaving for home on the mail boat Saturday noon, who thanked him for the trouble he had taken in the matter, and for his honorable conduct throughout, Mr. Graves said, " I promised that you should have the boy on free territory, unmolested, and I have kept my word. I was satisfied a foul wrong had been committed, and I have done what I could to right it. I only hope the laws of New York will be equally prompt in punishing the guilty party.

" Honor to whom honor is due," and surely in this case the Kentucky slaveholder appears in high and honorable contrast with the " religious church " member from the North.

After selling young Hite, and getting his $500, Van Tuyl returned to Dayton, Ohio, from which place he wrote a letter to a lady in Geneva, which letter was intercepted. Supposing his villainy to be undiscovered, he came to Niagara Falls, N. Y., and there was arrested and taken to Geneva. " He was met at the Geneva railroad station," says the *Albany Journal*, " by an immense crowd of intensely excited and indignant citizens, most of v hom were black, and, but for the presence of a number of officers, would probably have been subjected to harsh treatment." " As it was," says the *Cortland Republican*, " one colored girl aimed a blow at his head with a bar of iron, which fortunately shattered a lantern into a thousand pieces, instead of laying open his skull."

Prue was summoned as a witness from Ohio, and a purse was raised there to enable him to return.

Of Van Tuyl's release we find no account, but in the following April (1858), we find him in New Orleans, where he was recognized by the Kentuckian to whom he sold the boy Hite. Van Tuyl there went by the name of Edwin Read. He was arrested and taken to Kentucky, and being tried at Frankfort, on a charge of obtaining money by false pretences, was acquitted by the jury. He was immediately handed over to New York officers, to be tried in that State for kidnapping.

Brooklyn, New York. A man, nearly white, owned as a slave by a planter in Georgia, arrived at the port of New York on Saturday last, in the steamship Florida, from

Savannah. The captain was not aware that he was on board until he was several days out, and on his arrival in New York secured the services of two policemen, who took the man (who is called John Smith) to the house of Thomas McNulty, at Red Hook Point, where he was guarded night and day by four persons employed for that purpose. The fact became known to Mr. Lewis Tappan, who applied to Judge Culver, of the Brooklyn City Court, for a writ of *habeas corpus*, which was granted. Constable Oliver served the writ, and brought the fugitive before the Judge, at his house in Williamsburg, where the case was disposed of, and it is understood that he was discharged. It is also understood that an action will be commenced against those who retained Smith in their custody. Smith was to have embarked for Georgia yesterday. It is not probable that he went in that direction: — *N. Y. Tribune.*

☞ A fuller account of this case may be found in the *Anti-Slavery Standard* of Dec. 12, 1857.

Wholesale Capture of Fugitives in Nebraska. The St. Joseph (Mo.) *Gazette* relates the following account of a wholesale capture of runaway negroes :—

During the past week, we heard, through a gentleman living near this city, the following interesting account of the capture of *eleven* runaways :

About a fortnight since, a gentleman stayed at our informant's house on his return from Iowa, whither he had been in pursuit of the fugitives above alluded to. The negroes made their escape from Clay, Jackson, and Platte Counties several months since, and have eluded all pursuit until the last three weeks. The gentleman of whom we speak, we believe, lives in Clay or Platte, and owns five of the negroes. He relates that he first heard of them at or near Topeka, Kansas, some time since, whither he went to capture them. The people of that famous burgh succeeded in defeating his efforts to get his property. He then applied to the authorities for a force which was sufficient to effect his purpose. When this was ascertained, the negroes were secreted and assisted to again escape. He then hired a free negro of Jackson County to pursue them. This fellow being shrewd, and having some knowledge of the character of an

Abolitionist, went to Topeka and represented himself as a fugitive. This he knew to be the key to the hearts of negro lovers. A horse was furnished him, and information given where he might join the party he was in quest of.

The master, after receiving this information, again made pursuit, and overtook his negroes, in company with six others, about two weeks since, in Iowa, in a bend of the Missouri River near Nebraska City. In company with three other gentlemen, he proceeded at once to capture them, as they had determined upon resistance. The leader of the negroes fired three times without effect, when he was shot down. The other negroes were summoned to give up their arms, when they threw down *thirty odd revolvers*, and surrendered themselves. The negro who did the shooting is the same who killed Myers, at Brownsville, under similar circumstances, some six months since. It is not ascertained whether he was fatally wounded or not. The whole party of negroes, we understand, passed through this city, under the convoy of their capturers, about two weeks ago.

Indianapolis, Indiana. A colored man by the name of West was recently several days on trial, before a United States Commissioner, as to his right to liberty, Dr. Austin W. Vallandingham, of Frankfort, Ky., claiming him as his chattel. This claim was established to the satisfaction of the Commissioner, Ray, who gave him up to Kentucky slavery. Subsequently, the case was brought before Judge Wallace, of the State Court, who decided that the Commissioner's writ was the paramount law of the land in the case, and the poor fellow was sent back to Kentucky, under guard of United States officials, and at United States' expense.

While the trial was in progress, Dr. Vallandingham had his chivalric nerves somewhat shocked by an arrest for kidnapping, and that, too, on the affidavit of Samuel Williams, a colored man. On this charge, he was brought before the Mayor, who required bonds for his appearance for trial at a later day — and at the time of trial, finally released him. The only defence set up was that Williams, being a colored man, was not competent to file an affidavit or give evidence against a white man, the Constitution of the State of Indiana prohibiting the testimony of such persons !!

Thus, by a decision of a State Judge, corroborated incidentally by the Mayor of Indianapolis, the sovereignty of Indiana is laid in the dust beside that of Ohio, and the dictum of a fugitive slave Commissioner is recognized as the supreme law of the land. Thus does a miserable slave oligarchy rule in our State capitals, as well as at Washington; and our enslaved and mammon-worshipping people love to have it so.—*Ohio Bugle*, Dec. 12, 1857.

The Indianapolis *Journal* gives the following account of the termination of the case :—

" About half-past five o'clock on Saturday afternoon, the negro West was taken from the Democratic head-quarters at the Palmer House to the Union Depot, and placed in the room above the ticket office, to wait for the departure of the Jeffersonville train. A little before 7 o'clock, the negro, with a slavery-loving Democrat having hold of each arm, one pushing him behind, another pioneering the way, with thirty or forty others making the 'body guard,' was brought down the stairs and placed on the train. Like a wild beast when he is caged, the negro was shoved in, thrust into a seat, and the blinds let down to prevent the crowd from looking into the car.

A large crowd was present to see the exit of West out of the city. No demonstration was made towards preventing the Marshal and his posse from putting the negro aboard the train. Smiles of contempt played upon the faces of many who witnessed the loyalty of the distinguished posse of the Marshal."

West arrived at Louisville, Ky., on Sunday night, and was immediately placed in jail for safe keeping.

Ann Arbor, Michigan. Several detectives, among whom we have only the names of Officers Sprague and Wilcoxson, took a supply of small arms, handcuffs, &c., and went to Ann Arbor for the purpose of catching a couple of fugitive slaves there. They had arranged for an amicable partition of the reward. Not being able to keep their errand quite to themselves, word was got to the poor fellows, who were at work in a field, and they betook themselves forthwith to a place of greater security.—*Detroit Tribune.*

Slave-Hunting in Kansas. Another of those outrageous and tyrannical acts which are peculiar to the slavery-fostering

government of the United States was perpetrated in this
town on the night of Wednesday last. A file of soldiers, at
the dead of night, were marched up to the residence of Mr.
John Richey, immediately on the outskirts of the town,
headed by that pusillanimous tool of bogus law and slave-
catchers, Deputy Marshal Butcher, who, it will be remembered, made us a similar visit about three weeks ago. The
object of this visit, as before, was to capture some alleged
fugitive slaves, whom the Deputy, and one Mills, their pretended owner, believed to be secreted here.

Without presenting a writ or other evidence of his acting
in any official capacity, the Deputy, true to the instincts of
that Border-Ruffianism which he serves, attempted at once
to forcibly enter Mr. R.'s house, by breaking open the door
with an axe, but was brought to a stand by the click of some
sharp-shooters, and was compelled to obtain an increased
force to secure an entrance. It is needless to say that no
"niggers" were found. The Garvey House was afterwards
searched by them, with the same result.

How long our citizens are to be harrassed in this way, the
sanctity of their dwellings outraged, and themselves subjected
to pillage and insult, is a question yet to be answered. Its continuance or cessation depends entirely upon the answer which
the people themselves shall give to it. Time was, when a
man's house was his castle, into which no power could venture
with impunity, without due process of law. Shall that time
ever return? It is for the people of Kansas to say whether
a band of assassins and mountebanks, who pretend to ad-
minister law in this Territory, shall continue to desecrate their
dwellings, prostitute justice, and set at nought the most sacred
and inalienable of rights. Let Deputy Marshal Butcher, or
any other man who shall attempt to violate the sacredness of
the home circle, as has been done in this instance, feel at once
the vengeance of a sovereign citizen, and the extent of the
peril which he thereby incurs.— *Topeka Tribune, in Bugle,*
Dec. 19, 1857.

Ann Arbor, Michigan. Two men from North Carolina
spent much time in efforts to secure two negro brothers,
called Tom and David, living in the neighborhood of Ann
Arbor. The brothers, suspecting the plot, went over into

Canada, where, it is said, their "owner" visited them, and endeavored to persuade them to go with him; but not succeeding in his plan, he left and returned home.—*Detroit Free Press.*

Philadelphia; Case of Jacob Dupen. Jacob (30 years of age) was arrested, near Harrisburg, by Deputy Marshals Jenkins and Stewart. He was in a field ploughing, and made no resistance. He was taken to Philadelphia, and on the morning of December 18, 1857, brought before Judge Kane. The only witnesses examined before Judge Kane were Thomas John Chew, of Calvert Co., Md., and Officer Stewart. Chew testified that he knew the boy Jacob—that he was the slave of Wm. M. Edelin, of Baltimore Co., Md.—and that he knew him 14 years in that county. Officer Stewart testified to making the arrest, and to contradictory statements made by Jacob.

Judge Kane (to fugitive)—Jacob, do you hear what is said?

Jacob—Yes.

Judge—Do you want to ask him any questions?

Jacob—I don't know what to ask him.

Judge—Well, does he tell the truth?

Jacob—I don't know what he said.

District Attorney—Was Mr. Edelin your master?

Jacob—Yes, sir.

District Attorney—Do you want to go home with him?

Jacob—I want to go somewhere.

District Attorney—Who brought you from home?

No answer.

District Attorney—Don't you want to answer?

No answer.

Judge—You are not obliged to answer. Where did you live in Maryland?

No answer.

Judge—Was it in Calvert County?

Jacob—Yes, sir.

The necessary papers were then made out, and Jacob was handed over to the custody of his master. There was no excitement in the court-room; indeed, no one present, except the officers of the Court and the parties.

At this stage of the case, Wm. M. Bull, Esq., came into Court, and stated that he had been employed by the friends of Jacob to defend him.

Judge Kane remarked that the case had been heard, and that he had remanded the fugitive to the custody of his master.

The counsel asked if it was not unusual for cases to be heard at so early an hour in the morning?

Judge Kane — There is no rule of Court which fixes a time for the hearing of cases. In the fugitive slave cases, there is often an attempt made to interfere with the execution of the law, and for that reason, they should be peremptorily heard.

Mr. Bull — That is the case, your Honor, in others besides fugitive slave cases. I did not know that in any case the defendant had not a right to be represented by counsel. — *Philadelphia Bulletin*, Dec. 18, 1857.

What a mockery of law was this, to say nothing of justice! What a sight it was, indeed, to witness this Judge and District Attorney helping each other to get admissions from the lips of this poor fellow, who had neither friend nor counsel to advise him, — and whose case was hurried indecently to its end, — violating even the Fugitive Law itself, in obtaining and using the accused man's witness to his own harm! Here was a gross violation of the rights of the fugitive; — enough to have caused the impeachment of both officers. The Judge, even while informing the accused that he is not obliged to answer, urges and shapes his questions to extort from the friendless man an admission that he had lived in a slave State. Dark days were these, when on the side of the oppressor there was power, and men in high places did wickedly, and no man cared for the oppressed.

DAVID W. BELL and son, of Indiana, were forcibly abducted from their home and carried across the river into Kentucky, on suspicion of having aided the escape of a slave belonging to a Mr. Ditto. The kidnapping men first came to Mr. Bell's house as friends, and were entertained there. Having thus played the part of spies, and laid their plans, a posse of Kentuckians was brought across the river from Brandenburg, and at 10 o'clock at night they forcibly carried them to Kentucky, and lodged them in jail. — *Indiana State Journal.*

After they had lain in Brandenburg jail nearly a year, two other sons of Mr. Bell, lately returned from California, went across the river, on a day when the men of Brandenburg were mostly absent at a barbecue, demanded the jail keys, took out their father and brother, armed them with revolvers, and all succeeded in getting safely over to Indiana, though pursued by nearly twenty persons. — *Standard*, August 28, 1858.

Slave Chase in Nebraska Territory. Sometime in 1857, three colored men passed through Nemaha City northward. Some persons suspected them to be fugitive slaves, and having no better business than to be kidnappers' hounds, collected a party of men, who, on horse and mule-back, followed their prey, and overtook them. " One negro was shot through the right arm by two white men, and captured, because he could not swim the Missouri River. The other two negroes shot William Myers and killed him, and finding themselves surrounded, without hope of escape except by an extraordinary movement, seized, mounted, and rode off two of the enemy's horses. Neither horses nor negroes have been recovered. The wounded negro was detained in jail in Nemaha County, at an expense of about $300, until our recent November term of the District Court, when, upon affidavit, his trial was transferred to Otoe County ; and there, about a week ago, the poor negro, with one arm, was returned to his master without a trial."— *Nemaha City Journal*, January, 1858.

Sandoval, Illinois. "Three well-dressed and manly-looking negroes were arrested at Sandoval, at the junction of the Illinois Central and Ohio & Mississippi Railroad, last week, and locked up in the Salem jail. They were supposed to be fugitive slaves. Notice of their capture being given, a man calling himself their ‘ master ' appeared, and took them in charge, as we understand, without process of law, and carried them to Missouri and bondage."— *Chicago Tribune*, January 25, 1858.

Free man kidnapped from New York. Under date January 24, 1858, the Mayor of Richmond, Va., (Joseph Mayo, Esq.,) wrote to the Mayor of New York, saying that a man named Mason Thomas had been brought before him, charged with kidnapping from New York City a negro named George

Anderson, and selling him as a slave; and that Anderson, being questioned, said he was a free man, and had been hired by Thomas in New York, to work for wages in Pennsylvania. The Richmond Mayor desired evidence, if it could be had, of the truth or falsehood of Anderson's story. Mayor Tiemann, of New York, caused the needful inquiries to be made, when it was found that George Anderson's account of himself was "correct in every particular." The necessary papers, affidavits, &c., were immediately forwarded to Richmond. — *Standard*, February 6, 1858.

Gov. King, of New York, sent officers to Richmond, with a requisition for both Thomas and Anderson; they were delivered up, and brought to New York. Thomas, in default of bonds, was imprisoned to take his trial for kidnapping.

Case of WILLIAM M. CONNELLY, *of Cincinnati.* "On Monday of last week, as Deputy Marshal Elliott, of this city, was on his way home from Washington, he stopped in New York City, and requested Marshal Rynders, of that district, to aid him in the arrest of William M. Connelly, who is under indictment here for harboring the slaves of Col. Withers, of Kentucky, while they were in this city in June last. The Marshal designated one of his deputies, named O'Keefe, who was to meet Elliott at 7 o'clock in the evening, to proceed to the office of the daily paper upon which Connelly was employed as a reporter, to make the arrest. O'Keefe went to the office in advance of the time agreed upon, and sent to an upper room for Connelly. The latter came down at once, and the arrest was made. Connelly expressed his willingness to accompany the officer, but requested permission to return to his room to arrange his papers. He was permitted to do so, the officer remaining below, who, after waiting a reasonable time, and the prisoner not returning, proceeded to the upper room, and found that Connelly had made his escape through another entrance into the street, and has not since been heard of. Marshal Rynders has offered a reward of $50 for his arrest." — *Cincinnati Gazette*, February, 1858.

Connelly was subsequently arrested, and taken to Cincinnati; he was tried and convicted in May, although it was proved that the slaves in question had been in the habit of coming to Cincinnati with their master's consent, thus becoming free by the laws of Ohio. Mr. Connelly was fined ten dollars, and to be imprisoned twenty days; — not even Judge Leavitt venturing a severer sentence.

Kidnapping at Pittsburg, Penn. The Pittsburg *Post*, of February 13, 1858, and other Pittsburg papers of that time, represent that, some five years previously, a light mulatto man, named George W. Farris, escaped from his master, a wealthy planter by the name of Reiglan, (in some accounts called Ruggles,) near Tuscumbia, Alabama, said master being also the reputed father of Farris. He was a fine mechanic, came to Pittsburg, married, and settled. A fellow mechanic, named George Shaw, who had worked on the same plantation with Farris, followed him to Pittsburg, and endeavored to entice him back into the slave States, but without success, until about a year since, when, by showing him a forged letter or letters, he induced him to go to St. Louis, and from there, to a small town named Brunswick, to work as a bricklayer. Here Farris was arrested by the United States authorities, and carried back to Alabama. Farris's wife (a white woman) remained in Pittsburg, with one child, a little girl of three years old, white, and attractive. Soon the mother had reason to think that Shaw was planning to get possession of her child, with a view to carrying her also into slavery, being in league, for that purpose, with a man named Cassel, employed at the Pittsburg Theatre; and, on her complaint before the Mayor, Shaw and Cassel were arrested, and held for trial. Shaw had boasted that he had been in pursuit of Farris for five years, and had received considerable sums of money in payment for his services. His principal employer seems to have been a son of Reiglan the elder — consequently a half-brother of Farris, against whom the villainous plot was laid. This statement Shaw had made to John B. Nessle, of Lowellville, Ohio, as was declared by a correspondent of the Pittsburg *Gazette*, in a letter dated February 22d. He told Nessle he had received five hundred dollars and his expenses, being then on his way home from Tuscumbia, where he had been to deliver up Farris.

The Pittsburg *Gazette* of February 16 gives further particulars, from which the following is taken: —

"We noticed in brief yesterday morning the case of a man named Farris, who used to work in this city, having been entrapped by a wretch named Shaw, and returned to the hands of a slave-driver named Raglan, or Ruggles. George W. Farris was a white man, to all appearance. He married a white woman, and being a skillful mechanic, was able to earn a good living. He is one of the men you may meet every day at the South, bought and sold like old shoes, who perhaps have a right to claim some Colonel, or General, or Senator, for a father. These great men have a natural horror for all Abolitionists, because the Colonels, &c., &c., do say that the 'Abolitioners' are in favor of amalgamation! Humph! His wife's maiden name was Mary Ann Wickham, and her mother now lives in this city, on Fifth street. In March, last year, Farris and his wife separated, he going to St. Louis, with a troupe of singers. His wife had one child, a daughter, by him, which is said to be very fair, and even beautiful, now three years of age. The man Shaw, who is now arrested in this city, charged with attempting to kidnap this child, as it is alleged he has the father, and returned him to this Raglan, or whatever his name may be, in Alabama, is said to be the same who made some excitement here over two years ago, (in July, 1855.) He was at that time arrested on the premises of Mrs. Gardiner, in the 9th ward, with matches, augurs, chloroform, and all the necessary arrangements for burglary and plunder. He appears, from boasts he has made and from facts that have transpired in reference to his actual thefts and this attempted one, to belong to the class of pimps, burglars and slave-catchers, one equally as honorable as the other."

Shaw remained in jail in Pittsburg, unable to find bail, until the autumn, when he was tried and found guilty on four of the six counts of the indictment.

This case, like others in these pages, shows how closely allied the hunting of fugitive slaves is to the stealing of free persons, adults or children, colored or white.

Kidnapping in New York City. James P. Finlay, *alias* Haley A. Howard, (said to be a Canadian,) and his reputed wife, Anna Brainard, *alias* Anna Howard, made an attempt (which came near being a successful one) to kidnap and sell as a slave, a colored girl named Sarah Harrison, the daughter of poor but respectable parents living in New York, corner of Baxter and Broome streets. They pretended they wished the child to go and live with them as a servant in Newark, N. J. She went with them in the cars, but instead of stopping at Newark, they took her directly to Washington, where they arrived the next morning, March 9th. It is alleged that Finlay immediately offered the girl to a slave-driver in that city for $600, but it appears did not make a bargain.

The girl, having become alarmed, went to Mr. Willard (Willard's Hotel) and claimed his protection. The kidnappers, thus exposed, suddenly left for Baltimore, and Mr. Willard opened a correspondence with the Mayor of New York, and soon obtained proof of the truth of the girl's story. Gov. King sent a requisition to Maryland, and Finlay and his wife were arrested at Ellicott's Mills and brought back to New York. Dr. C. F. Clay, of New York, was also arrested as an accomplice. He at first denied all knowledge of the matter, but subsequently made a full disclosure of the plot.

The above account is obtained from the *Evening Post* of March 24, and the *Standard* of April 3, 1858.

Finlay was sentenced to two years' imprisonment in the penitentiary; but, when about eight months of the sentence had expired, was pardoned out by Gov. Morgan, on the alleged ground that F. was a tool of others.—*Standard*, Jan. 29, 1859.

A Daring Attempt to Kidnap two colored women, and sell them into slavery, was made in Chicago by an Englishman named Thomas Radcliffe, stopping at the Massasoit House in that city. He had come from Toronto, bringing one of the women, named Hannah Blackson, with him, as his servant. The plot, however, was discovered by a man whom he (Radcliffe) had endeavored to make an accomplice.— *Chicago Journal.*

ARCHY, *at San Francisco, Cal.* This case, which created intense excitement in San Francisco, may be found fully detailed in the New York *Evening Post ;* also in the *Anti-Slavery Standard* of April 24, 1858. The principal facts in the case are these:—

A Mr. Stovall, of Mississippi, being in feeble health.

5

in 1857 made the journey to California overland, taking with him his slave Archy, 19 years of age; with the intention, as he announced, of returning to Mississippi again, after an absence of a year and a half, or thereabouts. On arriving at San Francisco, he hired Archy out for over a month. After the lapse of some months, Stovall proposed to send Archy back to Mississippi in care of an agent; Archy escaped, but was arrested again by an officer of San Francisco. The Chief of Police, however, refused to deliver up Archy, as a slave, to Stovall, who demanded him. On these facts, the case went before the Supreme Court of California.

To the surprise of all, Archy was ordered into the custody of Stovall. The *Sacramento Union* said: "The law of comity, — the operation of the State Constitution, — in fact, all the law of the case, was ruled against the petitioner [Stovall], and yet, because he is young, in bad health, and this being the first case, and the petitioner may not have been advised (! !) of the constitutional provision being in operation, he is permitted to take Archy back to Mississippi." ["O, learned Judge! Mark, Jew; a learned Judge!"]

Stovall attempted to take him away in the Steamer Orizaba, which sailed from San Francisco March (?) 5th. Great crowds assembled, and officers with writs for both Archy and Stovall went on board both the steamers which were to sail that day. But Archy was nowhere to be found. Presently it was rumored that he was concealed at a point down the harbor, and was to be put on board as the steamer passed. The officers remained on board, with boats and boatmen attending, and kept quiet watch as the steamer proceeded down the bay. Presently a boat was seen approaching the steamer, in which, as it drew nearer, the officers recognized Stovall, and, as the boat came alongside the ship, saw Archy also crouching in the bottom of the boat. Lees, one of the officers, sprang into the boat and seized Archy, whom he passed up to Thompson, another officer. Great efforts were made by a portion of those on board to prevent the officers from serving their writs, and Stovall and his friends threatened vengeance and violence; but the officers were calm and firm, and did their duty manfully. Stovall himself was next arrested, on a charge of kidnapping, and the officers, with their prisoners, returned to the city, — having received all needful help from the officers of the steamer.

On a writ of *habeas corpus*, Archy was taken before Judge Freelon, of the County Court, who ordered his discharge. But he was immediately re-arrested by the U. S. Marshal, Stovall swearing that he was a fugitive slave (!), had escaped from Mississippi (!), and fled into California (!).

Archy, at this point, screamed out at the top of his voice, " I'll die first — I's free man, sir — I'll never be carried into slavery." At these words, all order in the Court was at an end, and a general rush took place towards the prisoner. It was with the greatest difficulty, and in the midst of constant blows and fights, that the officers got Archy into the U. S. Marshal's office, — he himself resisting with all his strength.

Easton, Washington Co., N. Y. An attempt was made to take a fugitive man in this village, but it was foiled by the vigilance and united sentiment of the people. The intended victim was a large and powerful man. A correspondent of the Albany *Evening Journal* said : " Two of these slave *pursuers* are said to reside in Albany. For their benefit, and the benefit of all whom it may concern, I would say that said fugitive is here and intends to remain." — *Standard*, May 1, 1858.

Petersburg, Virginia. Five slaves (four men and one woman) sought to escape from Petersburg in the schooner Keziah, Capt. Wm. B. Baylis, of Wilmington, Delaware. The schooner had reached Norfolk, and was nearly out at sea, when overtaken by a steamer sent from Petersburg with officers, who searched the Keziah, found the slaves, and took all back to Petersburg, including the vessel and crew, which consisted only of the captain and mate. The exasperation of the mob was so great, that it was with difficulty that Baylis and the mate were got to the jail. — *Standard*, June 12, 1858.

Capt. Baylis was convicted, and sentenced to the penitentiary for forty years, — eight years for each slave found on board his vessel. Mr. Baylis is about 60 years of age. The schooner was confiscated.

☞ Capt. Baylis died in the Virginia penitentiary in the summer of 1859. — *Lynchburg Virginian.*

Sandusky, Ohio. " A colored waiter at the St. Lawrence Hotel, Sandusky, was, a day or two since, captured by a

Kentucky slaveholder, accompanied by a United States Marshal. They got him as far as the railroad depot, but the crowd of people who went along to witness his departure was very large, and got very much "mixed up" with the Marshal's party. In the confusion, the "fugitive" disappeared. The Marshal fired a pistol through a man's hat, whereupon he was arrested, and gave bail for trial." — *Standard*, June 12, 1858.

New Albany, Indiana. Mrs. Bonner, wife of Matthew Bonner, was arrested on a charge of selling a free mulatto girl, three years old, into slavery. The child had been brought from Vicksburg, Mississippi, by a white woman, who stated that its mother was dead, and that the child was free. The child was left with a Mrs. Haney, who subsequently gave it to Mrs. Bonner, who took it to Louisville, and sold it to a family, about to remove to Missouri, for $250. Suspicion arising, an officer went to Louisville, and obtained such information as led to Mrs. Bonner's arrest. She was allowed to go at large on $500 bonds, and at the appointed hour for examination was missing. The child had gone to Missouri, but its recovery was expected. — *New Albany Tribune*, June 10, 1858.

JAMES L. BOWERS, a Quaker, of Charleston, Maryland, on bare suspicion of having aided slaves to escape, (having been tried and acquitted of the act,) was inveigled from his house in the evening, on the pretence that a traveller had broken his carriage and required assistance, — was then hurried off to some woods half a mile distant, stripped, tarred and feathered, and then suffered to depart, but not until a promise to leave the State within twenty-four hours had been exacted. A colored woman in the neighborhood, named Tillison, on a like suspicion, had the upper part of her body tarred and feathered ; and a colored man, in whose house she was found, was severely flogged. This case, though not strictly a case under the Fugitive Law, is so clearly one of the multifarious spawn of that hideous and brutal enactment,— the shame of our land and of our people — as of necessity to have a place here, amidst kindred barbarities, lies, and villainies.—See *Charleston (Md.) News*, June 26, 1858.

In the *Anti-Slavery Standard* of July 24th are fuller

particulars, showing the above statement to be within the truth. The following persons had been identified, under oath, by Mr. Bowers, and were put under bonds, in $500 each, to appear at next Court: — George H. Handy, Josiah Ringgold, Harris Beck, William P. Francis, Isaac Perkins, Samuel Baker, William T. Baker, Frisby Brown. There were about thirty persons engaged in the outrage, but Mr. Bowers could identify only the above eight. In the *Standard* of November 6, 1858, may be found further notices of Mr. Bowers.

Attempt to Kidnap in New York. On Sunday morning, Aug. 8th, (1858,) says the *New York Evening Post*, a colored lad, named Isaac Moore, residing with his mother at 231 Second street, appeared at the Eleventh Precinct Station House, and stated that early on the previous Wednesday morning, he was accosted by a man in Houston street, who took him by force on board of the schooner Ann Ellis, then lying at the foot of Third street. Here he was confined in the hold of the vessel four days, with a plaster upon his mouth to keep him from making a noise. On Sunday morning, the captain sent him above for a glass of water, when he succeeded in making his escape. A police officer was despatched to the vessel, but she had left and gone to sea. The vessel was from Virginia. "The boy is full-blooded, very black, but intelligent."

Terre Haute, Indiana. An elderly negro passing near this place was arrested by some men from Evansville, "on suspicion," as they said, of his being a fugitive! The captive was taken to the jail, but the jailor refused to receive him without the proper writ. He was then taken to a U. S. Commissioner's office. While waiting, an attempt was made to rescue the old man from the kidnappers; but in the confusion, officer Jones slipped him away, and, it is stated, put him on board a wood-train going South, and, in connection with the Evansville man, carried him off. — *Terre Haute Express.*

Shawneetown, Illinois. Kidnapping and Murder. On *Sunday*, Aug. 15, 1858, a likely negro boy, some 18 or 20 years of age, was arrested as a fugitive slave by two or three persons, near this town, and brought here. The boy declared himself to be free, born in Vigo County, Indiana, and showed himself acquainted with persons and places in that vicinity. The mass of our citizens believed him to be free. His captors had no legal process, and they were told they could not take the boy away without a Magistrate's certificate. But notwithstanding this, the boy was forced across the river by his captors, with the assistance of a few others, in the face of the assembled crowd. The next day, it was reported that the boy had escaped and could not be found. The day following, he was found dead in the river, lying on the Kentucky beach opposite this town. — *Shawneetown Illinoian.*

THE INGRAM SLAVES, at Cincinnati. Two slaves, 22 and 25 years of age, escaped from Robert M. Ingram, (or Ingraham,) of Dover, Mason Co., Ky., on the 5th of March last, and succeeded in getting to Canada. In the latter part of August, they came to Cincinnati, with a view, it is said, of helping some eight or ten others to freedom. Their master was notified by a colored man, who knew their object, that they were in Cincinnati; he came hither, obtained a writ, and secured the services of Deputy Marshals B. P. Churchill and W. L. Manson, and others, who served a writ on the fugitives as they were about leaving the city for New Richmond. The victims were taken to the United States Court House, and Commissioner Newhall's services called for. He objected to examining the case at that hour of night, but Mr. Ingram insisted upon his right to an immediate examination; whereupon Mr. Newhall acceded to the demand, [Is not the North pliant and cringing enough to suit the South? What DO they want?] heard the case, ordered the slaves into the custody of the master, and they were immediately taken across to Covington and lodged in jail.—*Cincinnati Commercial*, August 28, 1858.

Kidnapping in Delaware. Two negro boys were entrapped by some persons in Sussex County, says the *Wilmington Commonwealth*, and, being secured, were kidnapped and sold into slavery in Virginia. They were traced to the neighborhood of Richmond, Va., and immediate measures taken for their release. — *Chester County (Pa.) Times*, September, 1858.

Creek Indian Kidnapped and Enslaved. A Creek Indian, whose father was a mulatto, and who was making ox-yokes at Quindaro, Kansas, was, when driving his team in Kansas, surrounded by a band of Missourians, and taken as a slave to Independence, Missouri. The Creek had a certificate of his freedom from the Indian Agent. — *Cincinnati Gazette,* Sept., 1858.

THE OBERLIN-WELLINGTON RESCUE CASE, so called, of itself makes a thick volume. In this tract, we can give but the barest outline of it, and must leave untouched many of its aspects. It was a long-protracted effort on the part of the United States Government, prostituted in all its branches to the service of slavery — that "sum of all villainies," which assimilates to itself all that enlist in its defence and service,— to harass and punish a large body of peaceable, moral, and highly respectable citizens of Northern Ohio, simply because they could not sit quietly down and see a worthy young man of their town snatched from all the privileges of his home and of freedom, by a ruthless gang of man-stealers. Among their number were several students of the College at Oberlin, one of the Professors in it, and the rest were citizens of the town and neighborhood, both white and colored.

On Saturday, Sept. 11, 1858, two slave-hunters came to the house of Lewis D. Boynton, near Oberlin, Ohio, and remained there over two nights. Monday morning, a son of Boynton, only twelve years of age, took the horse and buggy of his father and proceeded to the village of Oberlin. He found the colored man JOHN, sometimes called Little John, and told him his father wished to hire him to dig potatoes. The unsuspecting John agreed to go, and to accompany the boy back. When about one half a mile from the village, a carriage from a cross-road came behind the buggy, when the Boynton lad stopped, and the first that John knew of the snare set for him was to find himself seized from behind by the arms, dragged from the buggy, pinioned, and placed in the carriage between his *brave* Kentucky captors. Fortunately for the kidnapped John, he was recognized, while being driven rapidly away, by an Oberlin student who was passing, and who made haste to give the alarm along the road and at Oberlin. The Boynton boy returned to his father's house with a golden reward for his part in the inhuman betrayal of a fellow-man into slavery. Can it be believed, even in this slaveholding and demoralized land, that this same Lewis D. Boynton, the hired accomplice in this work of kidnapping, should have been selected and allowed to act as one of the Grand Jurors by whom the rescuers of John were subsequently indicted?

To return: a large body of Oberlin residents responded to the alarm-call, and in various vehicles and well-armed, took the road for Wellington, the nearest station on the Cleveland and Cincinnati Railroad. Their numbers increased as they went, and on arriving at W., they found the slave-hunters, with U. S. officers, at the hotel, waiting the coming of the train. U. S. Marshal Lowe produced some papers, and read them. The crowd demanded that the man be brought out. Some State officers assured the crowd that, if they would be patient, the U. S. Marshal and company should be arrested as kidnappers. But the afternoon wore away, and nothing being done, and a sight of the prisoner at an upper window being obtained, the crowd would wait no longer. A ladder was placed by which men reached the balcony, entered the house and gained the attic story; and the prisoner was borne out, and down among the crowd, in a very short time. "No one was hurt, not a shilling's damage was done, not a shot fired, and the boy saved." The Marshal asked if his life would be spared; and the answer was, it would be, provided he would not visit those parts on the same errand again. The rescuers returned home in triumph.

On the 8th December following, some thirty-six of the rescuers, having been previously indicted, fourteen of them appeared at the United States Circuit Court at Cleveland, to answer to the charge of "rescuing, or aiding, abetting and assisting to rescue, a fugitive from service and labor."

The following are the persons indicted: — *Henry E. Peck, James M. Fitch*, Ralph Plumb, Charles Langston, *John Watson*, John Copeland, *Simeon Bushnell*, Lorin Wordsworth, Robert Windsor, *James K. Shephard, John H. Scott*, J. Manderville, *Ansel W. Lyman*, Matthew De Wolf, William E. Lincoln, Jeremiah Fox, *Henry Evans, Wilson Evans, David Watson*, Eli Boyce, *Wm. E. Scrimiger*, Lewis

Hines, *James Bartlett*, James H. Bartlett, Abner Loveland, Matthew Guillett, Thomas Gena, Walter Sawles, William Scriples, Robert R. Cummings, *Oliver S. B. Wall*, Henry D. Niles, Daniel Williams, Chauncey Goodyear, Franklin Lewis, *William Watson*, John Hartwell,—thirty-seven in all. It was spoken of, in the Cleveland papers, as a very singular circumstance, that, although quite a number of Democrats were prominent in the rescue, and some boasted openly of the active part in it they had taken, yet not a single Democrat was indicted! "Why this discrimination?" they asked; and answered, "No man who has read the charge of Judge Wilson, heard of the conduct of Marshal Johnson, and known the circumstances under which Lewis D. Boynton was selected and served upon the Grand Jury, will be at a loss for an answer."

At 2, P. M., fourteen of the indicted persons, — all who were then present, (their names appear above in italics,) — were arraigned before the Court. Hon. R. P. Spaulding, Hon. A. J. Riddle, and S. O. Griswold, Esq., appeared as their counsel, undertaking their defence free of charge. Judge Spaulding announced that the accused were ready for trial, and requested trial immediately. This evidently disconcerted the District Attorney, Judge Belden, and he was obliged to admit that he was not ready for trial, and asked a delay of a fortnight to obtain witnesses from Kentucky. Judge Spaulding asked if it was "reasonable that citizens of Ohio should be thrown into jail, to await the movements of Kentucky slave-catchers." The Court, however, granted a continuance, and stated that the defendants would be held to bail in the sum of five hundred dollars each. "We give no bail, may it please the Court, and the prisoners are here subject to the order of the Court." Again, both Court and prosecuting officer seemed confounded; but, after consultation, it was decided to discharge the prisoners on their own recognizance to appear at the March term.

In the course of the winter, a young man, a student in Oberlin College, went to the neighborhood of Columbus to teach a school. His name was Lincoln, and he was one of the number (see list above) indicted for participating in the rescue. He is described by Prof. Peck as "a person of excellent character and deportment." One day, when engaged

5

in his school, he was summoned to the door by a man named Samuel Davis, ("a bailiff in the U. S. Court,") who informed him he had a writ for him, and produced handcuffs, which he proceeded to apply. Mr. Lincoln objected to being pinioned, said he should make no resistance, but would go with him at once. But Davis, who was one of the men who got badly frightened at Wellington, at the time of the rescue, insisted on putting the irons upon Mr. Lincoln's hands, and bore him away. He was taken 12 miles to Columbus, put in a foul cell, where vermin came, and no food given him until 3 o'clock next morning. To his cell came two or three visitors, to insult him ; among them, a man named Dayton, who also had been a helper of U. S. Marshal Lowe at the time of the Oberlin kidnapping. The next day, the said Lowe took Mr. Lincoln to Cleveland, where Judge Wilson discharged him on his own recognizance to appear at the March Court. These facts are from a spirited letter of Prof. Peck to the Columbus *State Journal*, copied in *Standard*, Feb. 5, 1859.

The Grand Jury of Loraine County unanimously found bills of indictment against Anderson, Jennings and R. P. Mitchell, of Kentucky, and Jacob Lowe, (Deputy U. S. Marshal,) and Samuel Davis, of Columbus, Ohio, for attempting to kidnap John Rice from Oberlin.

The trial of the indicted thirty-seven came on, in Cleveland, in April, 1859. After a trial of ten days or more, upon the single case of Lorin Bushnell, the jury brought in a verdict of guilty. The name of Mr. Langston was called next. The counsel objected to his trial going on before the same jury which had just heard and determined the case of Bushnell. Judge Wilson gave it to be understood that no other jury would be called. Judge Spaulding and the counsel then declined arguing the case. The Judge said the prisoners would be allowed to go on their *parole* to return on Monday morning. The prisoners declined to give either recognizance or parole, and were taken to jail ; where the officer declined to incarcerate them in the cells, but made them as comfortable as he could in his own house.

At this stage of the case, the prisoners applied to the Supreme Court of the State of Ohio for a writ of *habeas corpus*, to take them out of the custody of the U. S. Marshal. This was heard by the full bench, and the writ refused, on the ground, it would appear, of *comity* (*!*) to the U. S. courts. In this decision three judges agreed, the other two (Brinkerhoff and Sutliff) dissenting. A report of the decision may be found in *Standard* of June 11, 1859. For C. H. Langston's address to the Court, before sentence, see *Standard*, June 25, 1859.

As the time for trial drew nigh of the four "kidnappers," indicted (as before stated) by the Grand Jury of Loraine County, and they saw no escape for them from the Ohio Penitentiary, a proposition to compromise the whole matter was made, and agreed upon, — by which the United States agreed to abandon all the prosecutions against the rescuers, and the Ohio State authorities agreed to abandon the suits against Jennings, Lowe, Mitchell, and Davis, the arresting officers! *Law* and *Justice*, indeed! Thus terminated, in July, 1859, the Oberlin Rescue case.

WILLIAM BRODIE, a free colored sailor, of the Bark Overman, of New York, was arrested in Darien, Georgia, charged with assisting slaves to gain their freedom, and, after such a trial as Southern laws condescend to allow a black man in such cases, was sentenced to be sold as a slave for such a period as would suffice to reimburse the purchaser for the amount of his fine and the costs of suit—$535. " Mr. James B. Stripling, of Talbot County, Maryland, offered to pay this amount for sixty-five years of service, and the man was knocked down to him to be his slave — virtually for life." — *Standard*, Oct. 2, 1858.

New London, Conn. "On the 20th September, a vessel left Wilmington, N. C., for a port in this vicinity. The captain had paid three dollars at Wilmington, as a search-fee for fugitives; notwithstanding which, when six days out, a fugitive man was discovered on board. He had subsisted till that time on some crackers and cheese brought with him. On arriving at the entrance of Mystic river, the captain went ashore in a boat, to get an officer to take the fugitive in charge. On returning, the fugitive was missing, having jumped overboard and swam ashore. The captain then went to New London, six miles distant, to make efforts for his recapture, and saw the fugitive in a store. He took the negro prisoner, and led him to the U. S. Custom House, and brought him before Collector Mather, U. S. Commissioner. Judge Brandegee, of the Police Court, hearing of the case, went to the Custom House. Ascertaining that there was no claimant of the fugitive present, and no legal papers in the case, Judge B. asked the man if he wished to remain there or go free. The man expressed his strong desire to leave immediately. 'Go, then,' said the Judge. The Custom House officials attempted to stop him, but the crowd being large, their efforts were unavailing, and the man was seen there no more." — *New London Chronicle.*

Chicago, Illinois. Two fugitives from Missouri were closely pursued, and traced to a house on Madison street. While the house was watched, the two were taken out at a rear passage, secreted, and ultimately helped on their way. They were a man about 30 years of age, an intelligent mulatto, and his wife, about 19 years of age, quite light colored. They had been pursued nearly two weeks, and $700 offered for their capture. — *Chicago Democrat*, Oct., 1858.

Lowell, Mass. A man named Keyes brought two colored women, mother and daughter, to Lowell; the mother had been, in all but form, the wife of Jesse Cornwell, a Mississippi planter, and the daughter was his daughter. They had been left in Keyes's care, by Cornwell, on his death-bed. Cornwell charged him to take the two women to a free State, and there see them comfortably located. For this special service, Keyes was directed to take $5000, cash, $4000 of which were to be equally divided between the mother and daughter, and $1000 to be retained by Keyes for his own services. Instead of faithfully performing this last dying request of his friend, Keyes, as alleged and consistently testified by his victims, immediately on the death of Cornwell, took the mother and daughter, and hired them out at $100 a year for six years, when he finally brought them to the North, arriving in Lowell in May, 1858. Here they remained in Keyes's family under strict surveillance. Sometime in October, the two women appeared before Isaac Morse, Esq., and told their story and entered a complaint. Keyes was arrested and held to bail in the sum of $6000. Keyes claimed that Cornwell *gave* him the women,—a very improbable story, of which no evidence whatever existed. — *Lowell Vox Populi.*

☞ A compromise was made between the parties, the women consenting to it, on account of the difficulty of getting evidence from Mississippi, and because of their own want of means to prosecute the case. Keyes obligated himself to provide an annuity for them, and gave them a small tenement in Lowell.

CAPT. HORACE BELL, of Harrison County, Indiana, (whose father and brother were kidnapped by Kentuckians, lodged in Brandenburg jail, and kept there for nine months or more, and who were taken from the jail by two other sons, of whom Horace was one, as already related in these pages,) was seized in the street of New Albany, by several men, hurried across the river into Kentucky, and lodged in an interior jail, in Meade County. The citizens of Harrison County being extremely excited by this outrage, and there being every reason to believe that serious difficulties would arise, Capt. Bell was released on bail, and returned to New Albany, October 29th. [Fuller particulars in *Standard*, Nov. 6 and 13, 1858.] — *New Albany Tribune; Ledger; &c.*

Harrisburg, Pa. " A young colored man, named Weaver, disappeared from Harrisburg some weeks ago, and has not been heard of since. There is a strong suspicion that he was kidnapped. The business of abducting colored persons and carrying them into slave States seems to have become quite common, and is said to be practised to a considerable extent in York, Dauphin, and Cumberland Counties." — *Standard*, Nov. 13, 1858.

Lawrence, Kansas. Two desperate attempts to kidnap two colored men, one a barber, named Charles Fisher, were made in Lawrence by a party from Missouri. One of the men was secured and carried some distance, but he managed to escape from a house, where he was confined in an upper room, during the night. Samuel Fry, a hackman, indicted as an accomplice, was released by Judge Elmore, on the ground that persons of African extraction are incapable of giving testimony. — *Lawrence Republican*, Nov. 11, 1858.

Zanesville, Ohio. A letter in the *Free South* gives an account of a hard and close chase after seven fugitives in that city, and of the colored people arming to defend their friends and themselves. — *Standard*, December 11, 1858.

Boston, Dec. 28, 1858. Brig W. Purrington, from Wilmington, N. C., was boarded by Officer Irish, with a writ of *habeas corpus* for a slave, alleged to be on board. The fugitive could not be found, however, and it was declared by the captain that, on the previous night (depth of winter!), he had leapt overboard and swam ashore, to Lovell's Island. For a more full account of this interesting case, see Boston *Bee* of Dec. 19th, and *Standard* of Jan. 8th, following.

Ten Fugitives from Virginia escaped in one company. They were pursued by a larger company of slaveholders, and overtaken in Pennsylvania, when a desperate conflict took place, one of the slaves interposing to save the life of his old master at the risk of his own; the slaves triumphed, and passed on through Northern Ohio into Canada. — *Painesville (Ohio) Telegraph*, December, 1858.

Nebraska Territory. Mr. S. F. Nuckolls came from Missouri to Nebraska, bringing slaves with him, and established himself at Omaha, opposite the Iowa shore. The slaves, finding free soil so near, thought they would venture over, and did so, — found friends, — were pursued from place to place, but succeeded in eluding pursuit. The outrages perpetrated in searching for these slaves exceed, if possible, in villainy and meanness, those recorded in most of the cases in this tract. Houses were entered, searched, torn down in revenge at their disappointment in not finding the slaves, — one boy was whipped almost to death, another boy was hanged and kept hanging till life was almost extinct, to "force a confession out of them." Canes and pistols were freely used, the slave-catchers declaring it their right to hunt for niggers wherever they thought fit. — *Omaha News*, Dec. 16, 1858; and *Chicago Journal;* in *Standard*, Feb. 5, 1859.

But the case had a sequel. In the Chicago *Press* of June 13, 1860, a year and a half after the occurrence of the above outrages, we find the following :—

" One R. S. Williams — of course a pestilent 'Abolitionist,

with just enough effrontery to maintain that he has rights that even nigger-catchers are bound to respect — seems not to have liked the proceedings of these marauders. He sued the would-be master, the owner of the flying chattels; and we see by an Iowa paper that he has recovered $8000 damages, in full, we suppose, for the insults and injuries to which he and his family were subjected by the barbarous clan. That's good. We like it; and if the same discipline could be enforced in the Egyptian Counties of this State, Illinois would make a new and long approach to freedom. We commend the case to the consideration of our friends in the Southern tier, where the nigger-catchers do most abound." — *Chicago Press,* June 13.

CHARLES FISHER, *at Leavenworth, Kansas.* He was the same man upon whom an attempt to kidnap was made in Lawrence, Kansas, as already mentioned. He had got employment as barber, &c., at the Planter's Hotel, in Leavenworth. In the night, his sleeping-room was entered by two police-officers, who, revolver in hand, threatened him with instant death if he did not yield. They handcuffed him, but instead of taking him to prison, put him into a skiff and rowed him across to the Missouri side. The cries of the kidnapped man aroused several persons, who were told "it was only an Irishman, who had been arrested for fighting." The next night he escaped from his captors, handcuffed as he was, got into a skiff, and floated three miles down the river. In attempting to land, he got into deep water, and was near being drowned; but "with the last effort of his failing strength, succeeded in reaching Kansas soil," and returned to Leavenworth. "A large meeting was held to welcome him back, and it was agreed on all hands he was worthy of freedom." He was, however, re-arrested, on charge of being a fugitive, and committed to prison. An attempt was made to serve a writ of *habeas corpus,* which was repelled by the officers of the jail; a second attempt was more successful, and Fisher was taken by Deputy Sheriff Boyle to the house of Judge Gardner. The *Leavenworth Times* of January 15, 1859, from which the above is taken, says that Fisher was a free man from birth. The *Liberator* of September 2, 1859, states that Charles Fisher was again entrapped, forced over into Missouri, and, after a cruel whipping, sold to the South.

[☞ An account of a remarkable interview had by J. MILLER McKIM, Esq., of Philadelphia, with the notorious slave-catcher, GEORGE F. ALBERTI, may be found in the *National Anti-Slavery Standard* of Feb. 19, 1859.]

THE DR. DOY CASE. *Lawrence, Kansas, Jan.* 27, 1859. A force of kidnappers, from Missouri mostly, but aided by certain residents in Kansas, carried off negroes from Oskaloosa, Kansas, to Western Missouri, as runaway slaves. Three white men, also, who were with the negroes, were carried off. These were Dr. John Doy, his son Charles Doy, and —— Clough. These last were examined, and, in default of the high bail of $5000, were committed to the county jail. None of these men had been to Missouri, and were in no sense "stealers" of the human property. A letter of Dr. Doy, in the *Leavenworth Times* of Feb. 14, (see also *Standard*, Feb. 26, 1859,) represents that, as he was conveying these negroes through Kansas, he and his party were set upon by ten or fifteen persons, fully armed and mounted, who, with pistols charged, captured and bound them. The principal actors in this outrage were Benjamin Wood, Mayor of Weston, Mo.; Fielding H. Lewis, Deputy Marshal at same place; Doctor Garvin, Postmaster at Lawrence, Kansas; Mr. Whitley (a Boston man), and two M'Gees, of Lawrence; and the notorious Jake Hurd, of Lecompton. They were brutally treated while in Platte County Jail. See Weston (Mo.) *Argus*, and Lawrence (K.) *Republican*. On trial, Charles Doy and Clough were released, but Dr. Doy was convicted. The Judge, however, granted him a new trial.

☞ On the evening of the 23d of July following, a company of resolute men came to the jail, and, by a stratagem, effected an entrance; they then told the jailor they had come to release Doctor Doy; the jailor saw he was in their power, and yielded. Dr. Doy's cell was opened, he came forth, and the whole party left before any alarm could be started. This bold act greatly exasperated the Platte County people, and a reward of $1000 was offered by the Sheriff for Doy's re-arrest, but without success.

Boston, February 19, 1859. A placard appeared in the streets, stating that Charles L. Hobson, of Richmond, Virginia, was in Boston, — named the hotel at which he was staying, — gave a very minute and certainly not "flattering" description of his personal appearance, and indicated the probable object of his visit, — the recovery of a slave who had fled from him. Said fugitive being in Boston, recognized the said Hobson one day in the street, accompanied by two neighbors, named Payne and Henderson. Hobson had offered, in Richmond, a large reward for the recovery of his *slave* — who was his own foster-brother. — D. Y.'s Boston letter in *Standard*, March 12, 1859.

THE UNITED STATES SUPREME COURT, early in March, 1859, gave a decision against the Supreme Court of Wisconsin, on account of its action in protecting SHERMAN M. BOOTH, who had aided in rescuing an alleged slave, Joshua Glover, from prison in Milwaukee, as already recorded in these pages. The United States Court unanimously decided that the whole course of the Wisconsin Court was totally illegal (!), and virtually revolutionary; that the Marshal had a right, and it was his duty, to resist by force any such interference on the part of the State powers (!!); and that the Fugitive Slave Act was clearly constitutional (!).

THE WISCONSIN SUPREME COURT immediately adopted several strong resolutions; among others, that it regarded the action of the U. S. Court "as an arbitrary act of power, unauthorized by the Constitution," and is "without authority, void, and of no force." — *Standard*, April 2, 1859.

In the autumn of 1859, the United States District Attorney appeared before the Supreme Court of Wisconsin, and made a motion that the mandate of the U. S. Supreme Court, (which reversed the decision of the Wisconsin Supreme Court, that the Fugitive Slave Law is unconstitutional,) be filed in the Wisconsin Court. Had this motion been granted by the Court, it would have, in effect, acknowledged itself in error in its previous decision, and submitted to the law as a constitutional one. The motion, however, failed, — Chief Justice Dixon favoring it, but Judge Cole dissenting, and Judge Paine (who had formerly been counsel in this case, arguing the law to be unconstitutional) being constrained to leave the matter in the hands of his colleagues.

SHERMAN M. BOOTH, the original defendant in this Wisconsin case, was re-arrested, March 1, 1860, by the U. S. Marshal for Wisconsin, in obedience to a process issued by the U. S. District Court, and imprisoned in the United-States Custom House at Milwaukee. The Wisconsin Supreme Court refused to release him by *habeas corpus*. Mr. Booth brought a suit for false imprisonment against U. S. District Judge Miller, and the Marshal, J. H. Lewis.

In the *Standard* of July 14, 1860, may be found Mr. Booth's statement of his own case; written from his prison in the Custom House. About the middle of July, another application was made to the Wisconsin Supreme Court for Mr. Booth's release, which was refused, the Court being equally divided. (See *Standard*, August 11, 1860.)

On the 1st of August, (a day consecrated to *emancipation!*) Mr. Booth was taken out of his cell in the Custom House by a small band of resolute and armed men, while a portion of his guard were at dinner, and the officer left in charge locked up in his stead. Means had been provided for conveying Mr. Booth immediately out of town. — *Idem*.

On the 8th of October, 1860, Mr. Booth was re-arrested at Berlin, Wisconsin; he was rapidly taken to Milwaukee, and again incarcerated in his old cell in the Custom House.

Is the Slave Power always to be omnipotent in America?

Southern Indiana. About this time (March, 1859), two fugitive slaves were captured, and taken to Louisville, Ky., and thrown into prison. They made a desperate resistance, shooting one of their pursuers, and wounding him so badly as to make his recovery doubtful. One of the negroes was shot in the shoulder, and otherwise injured by blows. The slaves were said to be from South Carolina.

MASON BARBOUR, *near Columbus, Ohio*, 45 years of age, arrested as a fugitive, by U. S. Deputy Marshal Jacob K. Lowe, — brought to Cincinnati, — the needful papers obtained, — and then taken to Kentucky by Lowe, and delivered up to his *owner*, a Virginian named Absalom Ridgely, living about 20 miles from Wheeling. — *Cincinnati Press*. March 26, 1859.

LEWIS EARLY, *Cincinnati*. "In April, 1856, a negro named Lewis Early left the premises of George Killgore, of

Cabell County, Va., and came to Ohio, and has since been at work in this State, a part of the time for Mr. Robinson, a relative of Mr. Killgore's, residing in Ross County, in this State. On the 17th of January last, Mr. K. gave to his son, James Killgore, residing in Kentucky, a power of attorney to pursue and bring back the fugitive. With this view, a new warrant was procured from Commissioner Charles C. Brown, of this city, armed with which document, Deputy U. S. Marshal Manson, accompanied by Mr. Killgore and another party, proceeded to Ross County, and effected the arrest. The negro was found chopping wood for a farmer, in company with another colored man, who immediately mounted a horse and gave the alarm that Lewis had been kidnapped and was about being conveyed out of the State by force of arms.

"The party then started on foot for the nearest station. Arrived in Buckskin township, Ross County, they were met by a constable and a large posse of men, armed with a warrant issued by Robert Coyner, Justice of the Peace, charging that 'three strangers' had kidnapped a colored man named Lewis Early, and commanding the officer to bring said 'three strangers' before his tribunal at once.

"The Deputy Marshal had no idea of contending against a force so much superior, and, with his companions, immediately submitted to the authority of the warrant, and proceeded to the office of the Justice, where he found a crowd of several hundred persons assembled. Justice Coyner demanded by what authority they sought to convey to other parts the body of the said Lewis. The warrant issued by the U. S. Commissioner was exhibited, and its genuineness satisfactorily proven, when Justice Coyner stated to the crowd that he felt himself bound to recognize the broad seal of Uncle Sam, and as his was an inferior Court, he should dismiss the charge of kidnapping, and set the prisoners free. This was accordingly done, and the Marshal, with the negro, succeeded in reaching this city by the train on Saturday morning.

The case is now in course of examination before Commissioner Brown of Cincinnati. The testimony, as far as taken, tends to show that the negro had been emancipated by a man to whom Killgore some years since gave a bill of sale of him."—*Cincinnati Gazette*, March 29, 1859.

DANIEL WEBSTER, *of Harrisburg, Pa., April*, 1859. "Assistant United States Marshal Jenkins, of Philadelphia, aided by Officer Taggart, attached to Recorder Even's office, and James Stewart, a police officer, all of Philadelphia, arrested a black man, about 35 years of age, near the Market-House, Harrisburg, on a charge of absconding from his master, a planter residing in the State of Virginia. He made a stout and vigorous resistance, and cried out lustily for help to save him, but no attempt was made to rescue him, notwithstanding there was a large crowd of people present attending market. The officers instantly took their prisoner down to the railroad, and got him into the Philadelphia railroad train, without molestation. Jenkins and the slave-owner had been here all the previous day on the look-out for Daniel Webster. He has a wife and two or three children, one of whom was buried last Sunday. He was a peaceable, honest, and industrious laboring man, and had been in the service of Senator Rutherford four or five years. This event has created great excitement, not only among the citizens of this borough, but also in the Legislature, where it immediately led to a warm debate.

On Monday, in Philadelphia, the case came up before U. S. Commissioner Longstreth. The excitement was very great, a large crowd being in attendance in and around the Commissioner's Office, among whom were many well-known anti-slavery ladies. The colored people were of course largely represented. The alleged fugitive was represented by Edward Hopper, W. S. Pierce and George H. Earle, and Benjamin H. Brewster, Esq., appeared on behalf of the claimant. Many technical and legal points were raised, and there was a good deal of sparring among counsel.

A long examination followed, continuing through the entire night, the ladies above-named sitting patiently all the while. The trial is very fully detailed in the *Standard* of April 16, 1859. From the report, as given in the *New York Tribune*, the following is selected:

J. H. Gulick objected to swearing on conscientious grounds, as he was a member of the Baptist Church. He said that the claimant in this case was his mother-in-law, and his wife one of her heirs. The cross-examination elicited the fact that the witness had been to Philadelphia, before the man was arrested, and submitted his papers to the Commissioner, who advised him to get others, as under those he would be compelled to release the fugitive. New papers accordingly were procured, and then the witness went to Harrisburg. He says :

"I first saw Daniel in Harrisburg on the 22d of February; did not speak to him ; did not wish to speak to him ; I stopped at Harrisburg for a day or two, for the purpose of spying out Daniel ; there was a rumor got up in Loudoun County in relation to Daniel's being in Harrisburg ; I concluded to spend an afternoon in Harrisburg on my way North ; I circulated around in the city, and while there I saw Daniel ; I stepped away after recognizing him ; did not want him to see me ; I called on Radebo, a constable ; he referred me to Snyder ; I could not find Snyder ; I then wrote to Mr. Rogers, my brother-in-law, telling him I had found Daniel, and if he wanted him, he might come after him ; when I returned to Harrisburg, I commenced circulating around after him ; was within one hundred yards of Daniel ; I said a great many things to the people to stop any excitement ; I said he was a burglar — at least, I intimated as much ; I was much confused ; I walked up to him, and discovering a scar, took hold of him."

The counsel for the prisoner, Mr. Earle, reminding the Court that the witness was a church-member, and of so tender a conscience that he could not take an oath, called attention to this deliberate lie, declaring that the man was arrested for burglary.

On Tuesday, the evidence for defence was brought forward. One witness, an intelligent colored man, swore that he met Daniel in Baltimore as a free man in 1848, in Philadelphia in 1849, and in Harrisburg in June, 1853. His evidence was straightforward, and was not shaken by a rigid cross-examination.

On Wednesday, the testimony being all in, the Commissioner said his duty as an officer was a plain and simple one, laid down by law. At an early stage of the case, he was satisfied that it was intended more as a show case, but he believed in the largest liberty of speech. After explaining his connection with the case before the arrest of the fugitive, which was merely in accordance with law, he said there were three things to be proved by the claimant, to wit : debt of labor, the escape of the slave, and his identity. He reviewed the testimony on both sides, and believed that the two first points were satisfactorily proven. He disagreed with the counsel of the claimant on the matter of the time of the escape. It was material in this case, and in evidence, that the claimant says that the escape was made in November, 1854, while it was proven that Daniel was in Harrisburg at least in the Winter of 1853, or the Spring of 1854. The power of attorney was also defective. In the point of the height of the negro, there was a difference of three inches. He confessed he was not satisfied with the identity. The prisoner was discharged.

The decision was greeted with immense applause. Daniel was carried on the shoulders of his friends through the streets amid a large crowd, intense excitement prevailing in the city. — *New York Tribune*, April 8, 1859.

COLUMBUS JONES escaped from Pensacola, Fla., in the brig Roleson, about the first of May, 1859. John Orlando, the mate, had the command of the vessel, which was bound for Boston, — the captain, Gorham Crowell, being at the time in Massachusetts. When some time at sea, Jones was discovered, and Orlando ordered him put in irons, and kept him twenty-four hours without food or water. On the voyage, he broke three sets of handcuffs, but was finally chained up in the caboose.

The brig arrived at Hyannis, Sunday, May 8th, and Orlando went on shore to communicate with Captain Crowell. During his absence, Jones got free from his chains, got into a passing boat, and had nearly reached the shore, when Crowell and Orlando, in another boat, intercepted him and took him back to the brig, representing that the people on shore were his enemies, and would return him at once to slavery.

A schooner named the *Elizabeth B.* lay at Hyannis, about to sail for Philadelphia. Crowell and Orlando applied to the captain of this schooner, Bacon by name, to go out of his course, and take Jones to Norfolk, Virginia, which Bacon agreed to do, it was said, for $500. The schooner sailed next day, with the slave on board, and got away before the people of Hyannis had learned of the matter.

The Roleson then sailed for Boston, and on her arrival, Crowell and Orlando were arrested and taken before the Police Court. They waived an examination, and gave bail for their appearance at the September term of the Superior Court to be held in Barnstable County.

Subsequently, the Grand Jury of Barnstable County returned bills of indictment against Crowell, Orlando, and

Bacon, and J. W. Baker, of Boston, owner of the brig. Caleb Cushing was retained as senior counsel for these men.

The trial came on at Barnstable, Nov. 15th, and lasted several days. But it suffices to say that the kidnappers were enabled to break through all the meshes of the law, and, notwithstanding the cruel act they had done on the very shores of Massachusetts, — an act abhorrent to every humane heart, — to get off free and clear, on mere legal technicalities! The shameless and craven doctrines laid down in the trial by Caleb Cushing are especially to be remembered. — See *Liberator*, June 24, Sept. 9 and 16, and Dec. 2, 1859.

JACKSON; *Zanesville, Ohio.* The emboldened men-stealers have again polluted the soil of Ohio, and borne off another victim. Jackson, the fugitive seized at Zanesville, had resided in Belmont County, Ohio, for the last three years. A few days ago, a miscreant named Honeycutt decoyed Jackson, through the agency of another negro, to Zanesville, where he was betrayed into the hands of Deputy U. S. Marshal Cox, who manacled him and bore him before U. S. Commissioner Cochran. The U. S. Commissioner immediately heard the case in his office, with the door locked, and remanded the negro to slavery. This secrecy added to the excitement, and after the prisoner was committed to jail, a writ of *habeas corpus* was obtained and served on the Sheriff, and the case was brought before Judge Marsh. After discussion by counsel, the Judge ordered the irons to be removed, and declared the prisoner at liberty. The *Courier* says:

"No sooner were these words out of the mouth of the Judge, than Mr. Cox, whose posse surrounded the negro, pounced upon him, declaring him his prisoner, &c., and calling on everybody present to aid him in keeping possession of him, &c. He was ironed and taken through the back door of the Court House to Fourth street, where a hack was in waiting, placed in it, and conveyed to the depot for the purpose of taking the train then nearly due for Wheeling — guarded by a large force of special deputies, all armed with loaded and cocked revolvers and other paraphernalia appropriate to their delectable occupation. A large number of blacks had preceded the carriage to the depot, and on its arrival there, an assault was made, with a view of rescuing the prisoner.

Many of the assailants fought bravely, but they were speedily dispersed — the bystanders, without reference to political preferences, voluntarily aiding the officers in maintaining possession of the fugitive. In the affray, every weapon that could be secured was brought into requisition, and clubs and stones were freely used on both sides, and some three or four shots were fired by the officers, but without serious results."

After the excitement at the depot, a writ of *habeas corpus* was served on the Marshal.

The *Cleveland Leader* says, — " The fugitive was held by the Marshal and his posse until the next morning, when he was placed on board a train and conveyed back to slavery, thus saving the Union ! " The *Courier* remarks :

" The only practical result of the proceeding, aside from sending a human being into life-long bondage, was the disgust inspired in the bosom of all intelligent and well-disposed people for an institution which required such disgraceful proceedings to sustain it, and to transform those who, for a paltry pittance became its willing creatures, into

" ' —— fixed figures for the hand of scorn
To point its slow, unmoving finger at.' "

— *New York Tribune*, May 10, 1859.

☞ For his action in the above case, Marshal Cox (said to be the father of Hon. S. S. Cox, M. C. from Ohio,) was expelled from the Baptist Church in Zanesville, Ohio, to which he belonged.

Five colored boys missing from Detroit, and supposed to have been enticed away by a lame white man, also suddenly missing. One of the boys was a son of William Jones, who is in the employ of the city. June, 1859. — *Detroit Advertiser*.

Free Man Imprisoned as a Fugitive. A colored man residing near Ottaway, Illinois, started for Pike's Peak in Kansas, being employed for that purpose by Mr. Aaron Daniels. Passing up the Missouri river, he was arrested and thrown into jail at St. Joseph's, Mo., as a fugitive from slavery ; and unless redeemed by friends, was to be sold to pay the jail fees. June, 1859. — *Ottawa Republican.*

EDMUND DAY, *of Salem, Ohio.* This young colored man, a son of Ellis Day, of Salem, Ohio, is "well known to most of our citizens, and was free-born," says the *Salem Republican.* Being in Cincinnati, and on board the steamer Glendale, he was seized by the mate of the steamer and two other men, on the pretence that he was a fugitive slave. He was thrown into the bottom of a skiff, held down by violence, and nearly choked; then taken to Covington jail. The next morning, he was taken by a Cincinnati officer back to that city, and efforts were made by his friends to commence a suit for kidnapping. June, 1859. — *Cincinnati Gazette.*

Mount Holly Springs, Penn. A respectable colored man was kidnapped at this place, and carried off into Maryland. June, 1859.

AGNES ROBINSON, *and child Mary,* were arrested in Washington city, charged with being fugitives from slavery in Maryland. They were claimed by one David Witmer, whose counsel was John H. McCutchen, and were ordered to be given into Witmer's custody by Judge Merrick. — *Washington States,* June 24, 1859.

See, also, article from *Intelligencer,* in *Standard,* July 9, 1859.

☞ On a trial in Washington County, Md., it was decided that she was a free woman, the case being tried by jury. — *Standard,* Jan. 21, 1860.

THE ANDERSONS, AND SCOTT; *Chicago.* The cool and deliberate villainy displayed in the conspiracy for abducting these men has its parallel only with pirates and friends of the Fugitive Slave Law.

Washington Anderson, 21 years of age, James Anderson, his brother, 18, and Henry Scott, "articles of personal property belonging to D. M. Frost, of St. Louis," left that city and came to Chicago to reside, — the last named having a brother in that city. Rewards for their apprehension, in all amounting to $2500, were offered. These rewards coming to the knowledge of two men, who had once been employed by the city as "detectives," they formed a scheme to entrap the fugitives and deliver them back, all three, into slavery.

6

These men were Charles Noyes and Charles W. Smith. They bribed a colored man, named Turner, and brought from St. Louis a boy, named Charles Oertman, who knew the fugitives and could identify them. Through Turner, Noyes and Smith got access to the Andersons and Scott, and commenced operations. Noyes pretended to be the owner of a large farm in the western part of the State, and desired to engage all three men to work for him; he offered tempting wages, and Smith, as his friend, was loud in praise of the many advantages they would enjoy. To make the thing work more smoothly, the colored men were taken round to various agricultural stores, where tools of various kinds, seeds, &c., were examined and bought, the men being consulted as to the best kinds, and allowed to select each his own hoe, rake, axe, scythe, &c., they appearing much pleased at the confidence placed in them. Thus influenced, they agreed to accompany Noyes, and went to his rooms, where Turner (acting as his servant) prepared a meal for them, and congratulated them on their good prospects. Meantime, Noyes and Smith hired an entire second-class car through to St. Louis, on the Illinois Central Railroad, for $150; and on the same night, the kidnappers took their victims on board the cars, bound for St. Louis. So quietly and skilfully had the thing been executed, that no suspicion had been aroused, nor were any inquiries started, until a private telegraphic despatch brought word that three fugitive slaves from Chicago had been landed on Bloody Island, opposite St. Louis. Subsequently, a colored woman arrived from St. Louis, who declared the three men to be the two Andersons and Scott, who were well known to her, that they were left on Bloody Island, and were there "cruelly whipped."

A few days later, Noyes and Smith returned to Chicago, and almost immediately, the former was offering for sale in the street a draft on St. Louis for $2350, — the price of blood! He soon obtained the money. But by this time the plot so craftily laid had been pretty thoroughly sifted and exposed. Turner, in great fear, had got himself placed in prison for safety from the vengeance of the colored people and others. Warrants were sworn out against Noyes, Smith, Turner, and Oertman. Smith and Oertman were soon arrested, Turner was already locked up, but Noyes, the leading spirit and special villain of the plot, "was unfortunately and shamefully allowed to escape capture, carrying with him the $2300." Officers of reputed vigilance pursued him. Before Justice Milliken, Smith waived an examination, and gave bonds in $3000 to appear at the Recorder's Court in August. Turner and Oertman, in default of bail, were committed to jail. The Illinois statute makes the offence in question KIDNAPPING, and the penalty imprisonment not less than one year nor more than seven years. But " the Democratic lawyers " of Chicago contended that, these being fugitive slaves, " there is no crime in taking them back to servitude." — *Chicago Press*, July 21, and *Journal*, July 22, 1859.

D. M. Frost, in a letter to the *Chicago Times*, pronounces the story of the " cruel whipping " entirely false. The whole letter may be found in the *Standard*, Aug. 27, 1859.

Zanesville, Ohio. Slave-hunters from Parkersburg, Va., sought a victim, or victims, in this neighborhood, but their " prey had escaped them." August, 1859.—*Zanesville Courier*.

A Negro Man arrests a White Man as a Fugitive. Near Edwardsville, Ill., on the Springfield road, one Isaac Dickson (a carpenter and white) was met by a negro, named William Brown, who presented a pistol at Dickson's head, and ordered him to yield. Brown, with the aid of a white man named Samuel Cobine, marched Dickson back to Edwardsville, and there informed him that he was arrested as a runaway slave, for whom a reward of $200 had been offered. Fortunately for Dickson, he was known to persons in E., on whose evidence he was released. The negro had been previously active in the work of capturing and returning fugitives. — *Edwardsville Journal*, August, 1859.

Cincinnati, Ohio, August, 1859. A negro boy legally free, and a resident of Cincinnati, was taken on Saturday evening, Aug. 27th, in the street, by two city officers, Slater and Leonard, and locked up in an engine house in Sixth street. He told them he was a slave, from Kentucky, and wished to be returned to his master. After a time, they came and took him to the river side, made a signal, and soon a skiff appeared, with a man in it, who proved to be Deputy U. S. Marshal

Butts, of Kentucky. The boy was placed in the skiff, accompanied by Butts and Slater, and rowed across the river, and placed in Covington jail. It afterwards appeared that the whole was a trap laid for the two officers, who had fallen into it; of which, being informed, they were greatly alarmed, and did not rest until the boy was brought back to Cincinnati. — *Cincinnati Gazette*, Aug. 30, 1859.

OLIVER ANDERSON, a colored man residing near Chillicothe, Ohio, was dragged from his own house on the night of October 12, 1859, torn from his family, and hurried off to Kentucky. The kidnappers were a Kentuckian and two Ohio negro-hunters. The Kentuckian claimed the negro as his slave; and in order to get away without molestation, he was put in the bottom of a wagon and covered with hay, while the claimant suffered himself to be handcuffed by his fellow kidnappers, who represented that he was a counterfeiter they were taking to Kentucky on a requisition from the Governor. The Columbus *State Journal* says:

"The kidnappers of Anderson were brought to trial, in Chillicothe, and were last week acquitted, on the principle of the decision of the Supreme Court in the Prigg case: That 'the master of a fugitive slave has the Constitutional right to pursue his slave into any State of the Union, and to recapture him, and to return him thence to the State whence he escaped, without process of law, State or National, and that he may call assistance, and use all necessary force on the slave, or other persons attempting to rescue the slave,' and any law which interferes with these rights is void.

"It is practically established, therefore, that any Southerner may come here, fix upon a 'likely negro boy,' or handsome girl, and summoning a force of ruffians to his assistance, may tear asunder all the ties of home and kindred, and carry unmolested his victim into hopeless slavery. It is not necessary that he should have any claim to his human prey under the atrocious fictions of Southern law. Let him say: 'This is my slave. Help me, you; and, you, stand back!' If the colored freeman resist, he shall be overpowered. If a white freeman interfere to save him, he may be shot down."

The *Anti-Slavery Bugle* of Jan. 21, 1860, gives the following additional intelligence:

"Oliver Anderson, the negro who was kidnapped at Chillicothe, on the night of October 12, 1859, and carried into Kentucky slavery, has demonstrated a problem in triunes. Oliver was unlawfully, infernally, and Deputy-United-States-Marshally dragged from his family and thrust into the bondage of negro slavery. But Oliver knew a thing or two, and instructed two fellow-slaves (one, his brother) in the knowledge, and one frosty night, the trio set their peepers upon the North Star, and their locomotive agents into action, and made tracks for Ohio. They reached the U. G. R. R. in good time, and were rushed through on the express train, getting to Columbus Friday morning. Don't start, brother Lowe! even your keen scent for human blood will avail nothing — the quarry is in Canada. This ought to be quite satisfactory to the managers of the U. G. R. R — two hundred per cent. on the original investment, and expenses paid by the kidnappers."

[The ever-memorable seizure of Harper's Ferry Armory, and town, in Virginia, by the brave and self-sacrificing Captain JOHN BROWN, and his little company, in behalf of the enslaved, took place on the night of the 15th of October, 1859.]

HENRY SEATON, a colored man, was seized in Cleveland, by Deputy U. S. Marshal Manson, mainly through the agency of a spy and traitor named George Hartman. The *Cleveland Leader* (Nov. 1859) states that Hartman stayed in the jail during Wednesday night, not caring to trust himself outside. The jail was watched by a party of negroes, who would have given him a rough reception if he had ventured out. Yesterday morning, about 9 o'clock, he left the jail as stealthily as possible, in the hope of getting to the New England House, where he boarded. Sharp eyes, however, saw him, and he was compelled to take refuge in Andrew's Saloon on Seneca street. This not being permanent quarters, he endeavored to escape through the back yard, but was caught by Andrew's big dog, which would have speedily disabled him, if he had not been called off. Hartman soon made his escape from here and succeeded in reaching the New England House, though closely followed by incensed negroes. Here he armed himself, and suffered no further molestation. He probably left the city upon the 7.40 Columbus train last evening.

The negro was hurried to Cincinnati, immediately taken before U. S. Commissioner Brown, and before it was known outside the court-room what was transpiring, the man was a captive on the slave soil of Kentucky. — *Cincinnati Gazette*, Nov. 12, 1859.

Kidnapping at Columbus, Ohio. " A mulatto man was seized at the railroad depot yesterday morning, forced on board the 8.40 train for Cincinnati, and carried off. The seizure was made by Deputy Marshal Jacob Lowe, who also holds the office of Deputy Sheriff of Franklin County, and Robert Mitchell, Constable of this city, and a number of helpers. No warrant or authority of any kind was shown. They told the bystanders that he had been robbing somebody. Although the man was seized by as many as could find a place to take hold, being a powerful man, he threw them off, and it was only after a contest that lasted, we are credibly informed, half or three quarters of an hour, that they succeeded in subduing him so as to force him into the cars; during the struggle, Deputy Lowe taking every available chance to hit him on the head with a heavy cane.

A colored man named Henry Alfred relates the following circumstances : — " He and Rice lived at Mount Gilead. A man by the name of D. C. Watson, who had been here several days, engaged Rice and himself to come to Columbus to be employed in a refreshment saloon that he was going to set up. They started together on Thursday for Columbus. The colored men stayed over night at Delaware, where Rice had relatives; but Watson came on to Columbus, and met them with the gang when they arrived in the morning. Alfred was not seized, but was roughly handled to prevent his interference. People at Xenia, where the train was due at 12 o'clock, were informed of the matter by telegraph, and we are advised that officers got on the cars there with a writ of *habeas corpus*, but were carried off.

" Alfred states that Rice had lived in the neighborhood of Mt. Gilead near eight years, and has a wife and one child there. Incidents like this among us leave no room for indignation or horror at John Brown's invasion." — *Columbus Journal*, Autumn of 1859. Also, see *Liberator*, Nov. 18.

Kidnapping Case, and Suit at Law. "Our readers will remember the case of a Marylander named Myers, who kidnapped some colored men at Carlisle, in this State, and carried them into Maryland, and who was afterwards arrested on this side of the Pennsylvania line and held to answer. At the November term of the Cumberland County Court, he was indicted for kidnapping, and put upon his trial.

"The three men arrested at or near Carlisle by Myers, who is a professional slave-catcher, were arrested upon the pretence that they were fugitive slaves, and were delivered to those who claimed to be their owners. Myers, after delivering them up, was enticed over the line, near which he resides, by a flaming handbill offering large rewards for more fugitives, and was there arrested by the Sheriff of Cumberland County. It was a part of the plea of the defence that he was enticed over by 'fraud and deception.'

"Upon the trial, which came off last week, it was proved and admitted that one of the negroes was the slave of Hoffman, of Frederick County, and that Myers was duly authorized to capture him; that he did so, and restored him to his owner. It was also proved and admitted that the two other slaves were manumitted in 1854 by the will of their owner, but that in February, 1858, the Orphans' Court of Frederick County, under the law of Maryland, passed an order directing the executor to sell them for a term of years to pay debts, and that shortly after the passage of such order, the negroes ran away; that Myers was duly authorized to take them, which he did, and restored them to their owner.

"The Court held, and so instructed the jury, that the question for them to try was whether in fact and in law the negroes were slaves when they escaped from Maryland; that it was proved that they were manumitted under rule; that if afterwards they went at large with the assent of the executor, such going at large amounted to an assent to their legacy of freedom, which made them entitled to their freedom in Maryland, on the authority of Fenwick vs. Chapman, and that therefore the defendant was guilty of kidnapping; that the order and decree of the Orphans' Court was conclusive evidence only that the negroes were ordered to be sold, but not that they were slaves, or that the court had any right to pass any such order. If the negroes were free, the decree would not make them slaves.·

" The jury was out for some time, but finally rendered a verdict of guilty. The conviction renders Myers liable to confinement in the penitentiary for not less than five nor more than twelve years, and a fine of not less than $600 for each negro kidnapped. He was convicted of taking *two*.

" The court and jury having decided that these negroes were free from the time of their arrest, the question arises, will the Governor of Pennsylvania demand their surrender as kidnapped citizens of this State? If they were white, he undoubtedly would.

" The Maryland papers talk of taking this case up on a writ of error to the U. S. Supreme Court ; but we do not see, exactly, how it is to be done. In the meantime, Myers will go to the penitentiary, where he ought to have been long ago. Whether the ruling of the court shall turn out to be good or bad law, the justice of Myers' sentence cannot fairly be questioned. The penitentiary is the right place for him and all of his tribe." — *Pittsburg Gazette;* in *Bugle*, Dec. 3, 1859.

At Chicago, January, 1860, "the Grand Jury of the United States District Court indicted eight citizens of Ottawa, Illinois, under the Fugitive Slave Law, for participating in the rescue of JIM, claimed as a slave, before Judge Catron." — *Standard*, Jan. 7, 1860.

The *Chicago Press and Tribune*, of Feb. 29, 1860, (see *Standard*, March 10,) adds that Dr. Stout and brother, and John Hossack, (who were among the number indicted,) were arrested and lodged in jail in Chicago. Afterwards, E. W. Chamberlain, Henry King, and Claudius B. King, all of Ottawa, were brought to Chicago and imprisoned. Their trial did not come on until October, when they were convicted of the " crime " of helping a man to his freedom, says the Chicago *Congregational Herald*, of Oct. 11th, 1860. John Hossack was sentenced to ten days' imprisonment, and fined $100. This carried with it costs of prosecution, said to be $591 more. Dr. Stout was sentenced to ten days' imprisonment, and fined $50 ; his costs were $802.21. C. B. King's sentence was one day's imprisonment and $10 fine and costs. Mr. Hossack and Dr. Stout were to lie in Cook County jail until fines and costs were paid. Dr. Stout was wholly unable to pay the amount for which he was held, and Mr. Hossack, though having some property as a farmer, has a large family to support. Mr. Hossack, on being asked by Judge Drummond if he had aught to say why sentence should not be pronounced upon him, addressed the Court in a very noble and truly Christian manner, taking the high ground of moral and religious obligation. His speech is published as one of the tracts of the AMERICAN ANTI-SLAVERY SOCIETY, in the same series with this tract. Mayor Wentworth, of Chicago, took an active interest in the case of Messrs. Hossack and Stout, and before long the whole amount necessary to pay their obligations was raised, and they were liberated.

JAMES LEWES, son of Abner Lewes, of Masten's Corner, Del., was caught in a lonely place, at dark, on his return home to his employer's, (Wm. Minner's,) by a man named Lemuel C. Morris, and kidnapped into Maryland. Here Morris tried to sell the boy to a Mr. Fountain. Mr. F., suspecting all was not right, told Morris to return in a day or two, when he should have his money or the boy. Inquiry being made, Fountain was persuaded of the boy's having been kidnapped, and wrote a note to his employer. The boy was returned, and Morris, who came for his money, was arrested and put in jail at Dover. — *Milford (Del.) News,* January, 1860.

Free Man Sold as a Slave. "The following particulars concerning the selling into slavery of a free negro were yesterday related to us by a legal gentleman, in whose hands the matter has been placed for the prosecution of the offending parties. Some time since, a telegraphic despatch was received by a detective officer of this city, [St. Louis,] requesting him to arrest and retain in custody a negro acting in the capacity of cook on board a steamboat plying between this city and Cincinnati. The despatch set forth that he (the negro) was a runaway slave, the property of a gentleman named Overton, residing about a hundred miles from this city. The officer fulfilled the orders, and placed the supposed runaway in jail. A couple of days after this, Mr. Overton came here and *identified* the negro as a slave of his; and afterwards placed him in the hands of a slave-trader, who disposed of him to a Southern gentleman named Wiseman, for a very round sum of money. Wiseman took the negro to New Or-

6*

leans, and there sold him for $3000. Shortly after this last transaction, it was ascertained that the negro was in reality *a free man*. He was born a slave in North Carolina. He afterwards moved, with his master, to Mobile, where he was emancipated.

"After his emancipation, he moved to Ohio, and engaged himself as cook on board a river steamboat. He left his free papers in Ohio, not dreaming, as he says, that any person would claim him as a slave. By some means, his emancipator heard of his enslavement, and immediately interested himself in his behalf. His free papers were taken to New Orleans, and by due form of law, he was declared a free man. Prosecution has already been commenced against some parties in New Orleans for being concerned in the selling of the free negro, and in a short time, suit will be brought against individuals in this State for the same offence. A legally gotten up warrantee deed was given to Mr. Wiseman, stating the negro to be a slave for life, and the same kind of instrument was produced by the gentleman who purchased him in New Orleans, as proof that he (the purchaser) had committed *no crime*." — *Missouri Democrat*, Jan., 1860.   See also *Anti-Slavery Bugle*, Jan. 14.

New York City, January, 1860.   A recently-arrived fugitive, weak from confinement and insufficient food on board a vessel, was found by a policeman in the street, who, supposing him intoxicated, took him to a station-house. Here the man imprudently confessed that he was a fugitive from slavery. Officer Terhune took him before Justice Brennan on a complaint of drunkenness, and then hurried to U. S. Marshal Rynders to inform him of the new slave case. As speedily as might be, Marshal R. sent a note to the Justice, desiring him to hold the prisoner, as he was a fugitive slave. But, alas! some friendly persons had just been before the Justice and paid the man's fine on the charge of drunkenness, whereupon he was discharged, and thus narrowly escaped the net spread for him.

"In consequence of this occurrence," says the *National Anti-Slavery Standard* of Jan. 28, 1860, "a Republican member of the Board of Police Commissioners introduced in that body a resolution to forbid policemen from engaging in the business of slave-catching. It was voted down, however, (!) so that the police, provided for this city [New York] by a Republican Legislature, is liable henceforth to be employed as an agency for the arrest of fugitive slaves. (!) "

Iowa City. " A miserable apology for a man, answering to the name of Curtis, was arrested in Iowa City on a charge of kidnapping. It was satisfactorily proved that he had undertaken to carry into Missouri, and there sell, *two free colored girls.* He was held in $1000 bail to answer the charge. These attempts at kidnapping are becoming common in the West." — *Standard,* Feb. 18, 1860.

Curtis compromised the case in Court, agreeing to adopt the two girls, give them his name, and educate them. — *Iowa City Republican;* in *Standard,* March 10, 1860.

Lawrence, Kansas. The *Lawrence Republican,* Feb. 16, 1860, details the circumstances of an attempt of " a pack of human hounds," — one of them being the infamous Jake Hurd,— to kidnap a woman living at Mr. Monteith's, in Lawrence. A sharp contest took place, resulting in the utter discomfiture of the " hounds." — See *Standard,* March 3, 1860.

Springfield, Illinois. A fugitive slave who was arrested in Springfield, and taken upon the cars for St. Louis by a Deputy U. S. Marshal and assistants, attempted to kill one of his captors, but failed. — *Standard,* March 3, 1860.

Kidnapping a Free Man in Pennsylvania. On the night of the second of March, 1860, a free colored man by the name of John Brown, residing in one of the tenant houses of J. Williams Thorne, Sadsbury Township, Lancaster Co., Pa., was kidnapped.

Four men entered his house at 10 o'clock at night, and commanded him to go with them, on a charge of robbing a store. No warrant was shown. Two of them gave their names as Gilmer Hull and Frank Wilson, neighbors well known by him, who assured him that no harm should come to him, but that they would return him the following evening. Being thus deceived, and naturally of a quiet, easy disposition, he permitted himself to be taken by the ruffians to a carriage, a few rods distant, without making any resistance or giving the least alarm.

Pursuit was made as soon as the alarm was given, and they were followed to the Mount Vernon Hotel, where it was ascertained that a carriage had passed, driving at full speed. Here the pursuit was given up, and nothing, up to the present writing, has been heard from them.

John Brown is a man of upwards of thirty years of age, large size and very dark, and is positively known to be a free man, having been raised near Downingtown, but has resided for many years in this vicinity.

Two arrests have been made, in the persons of Gilmer Hull and Frank Wilson, residing in the neighborhood, as aiding in the kidnapping. A hearing was had to-day before 'Squire Slocum, of Christiana, which resulted in the identification of the former by the wife of the victim. He was sent forthwith to Lancaster jail, in default of the required bail (six thousand dollars). Wilson was released. — *Standard*, March 10, 1860.

After several days' absence, Brown returned home. His story agrees with the foregoing in every essential particular. He further states that his captors said they should take him to Lancaster. Wilson said he would bail him and bring him back on the next day. He states that they took him out into the woods and put him into a carriage. Frank Wilson, with two other men, got in the carriage, and after going a short distance, Wilson got out. Before putting him in, they tied him. One of the men said he was his master, and would take him to Virginia ; they told him if he did not keep quiet, they would blow him through, and pointed pistols at him. Edward Mackey got into the carriage after Wilson got out, and they drove him (Brown) to McCall's Ferry, where they kept him tied in a garret, at Fisher's tavern, all the next day. Brown says he told Fisher he was a free man. Fisher replied, "Never mind, they won't hurt you."

In the evening, about 7 or 8 o'clock, Fisher came up into the garret and told the men who had Brown they might bring him down, "he had got the people all out of the barroom." They then took him across the river and on to Baltimore, in the same carriage they had started with. After reaching Baltimore, he was lodged in a jail, and left there for six or seven hours ; he was then moved to another jail, where the keepers asked where he was from. He told them he was raised in Chester County, Pa., by a man named John Baldwin, and that he was a free negro, never having been a slave. The keeper then said he would have nothing to do with him, unless they could identify him as a slave.

After he had been some time in this jail, a man by the name of Wm. Bond came in, who had been acquainted with Brown, and at once recognized him. Bond told the keepers of this jail, or slave-pen, that Brown was a free man, and prevailed upon them to let him go. They sent with him the following written statement:

"BALTIMORE, March 5, 1860.

The bearer of this, John Brown, is supposed to be a free man, brought here by some men, and offered for sale as a slave, and we, believing him to have been kidnapped, send him back to Lancaster County, where he says he came from.

JOSEPH S. DONOVAN."

Hull, Wilson and Mackey have been arrested. — *Lancaster Express.*

Hull was bound over in the sum of $5000 to take his trial for kidnapping. Fisher, also, the tavern-keeper, was bound over in $3000 to appear for trial at the April term. — *Lancaster Union,* March 21, 1860.

☞ In the following autumn, the barn of Mr. Thorne (the employer of the colored man in the above case, and who had been active in bringing his kidnappers to justice) was set on fire and destroyed, and it was with great difficulty that his house was saved from the flames. There were fresh tracks of horse and man near Mr. Thorne's barn, which, being followed, led to the house of Wilson, one of the indicted kidnappers, who was thereupon arrested on a charge of incendiarism. Hull and Wilson were convicted of the crime of kidnapping, and sentenced each to pay a fine of $200, (half to go to John Brown, and the balance to the county,) and to undergo imprisonment in the Lancaster County prison for the term of five years. — *Standard,* Dec. 15, 1860.

MOSES HORNER returned to slavery from Philadelphia, *April,* 1860. Is this the same case of which the *Anti-Slavery Bugle* of April 7, 1860, thus speaks? —

" A fugitive slave who was captured in Harrisburg was brought before Judge Cadwallader, of Philadelphia. for trial,

and by him adjudged guilty of being held to service or labor
in Virginia, under the laws thereof, and accordingly remanded.   An ineffectual attempt was made to rescue him ; but instead of giving to the poor fellow the liberty which the Dec-
laration of Independence says belongs to him, ten of the attempted rescuers were arrested, and committed to prison.
This will furnish business to the U. S. Courts, and add another to the many illustrations our history furnishes of the kind
of blessings the North derives from her ill-assorted union
with slaveholders and despots.   We shall learn the lesson in
time ; and though it may require many a flogging to beat it
into our brains, the South is no whit inclined to spoil us by
sparing the rod."

☞ In the famous LEMMON CASE, (recorded in the earlier
pages of this tract,) a decision was reached in the New York
Court of Appeals, in April, 1860, affirming the decision of the
Court below, whereby Jonathan Lemmon, of Virginia, was
declared not entitled to bring his slaves into the State of New
York, and hold them in slavery there, while on his way
from one slave State to another.   Five Judges concurred in
this opinion, — Denio, Wright, Wells, Bacon, Davies ; —
while three Judges dissented, viz. — Clark, Selden, Com-
stock.

ALLEN GRAFF and JOSIAH HAY were arrested in New
York city, and with much secrecy brought before U. S. Commissioner Betts, who ordered them into the custody of their
claimants, two men from Frederick County, Maryland.
Hay, on being brought up, appeared very much overcome ;
he sat, with his head leaning down on his breast, weeping constantly ; Graff seemed indifferent. — Standard, May 5, 1860.

CHARLES NALLE, claimed as the slave of B. W. Hans-
borough, of Culpepper County, Virginia, and to have escaped
thence in 1858, was arrested in Troy, N. Y., April 27th,
1860, and taken before U. S. Commissioner Miles Beach.
The examination was very brief.   Nalle was remanded to his
owner, and the necessary papers handed to the Marshal.
But some exciting scenes followed.   An immense crowd collected around the office, and at length Nalle, in charge of officers, came forth.   A fight ensued, the result of which was

that Nalle was rescued, through greatly bruised and his clothes nearly rent from his person. For a full and detailed account, see the Troy papers, April 28th, &c., and the *Standard*, May 5th, 1860. In this rescue, a colored woman was prominent, very active and persevering, until success crowned their efforts, — a woman known among the colored people extensively as " Moses," because she has led so many of their number out of worse than Egyptian bondage into the goodly land of freedom.

An effort was made in Troy to raise $1000, to be paid to the " owner " of Nalle. The Troy *Arena*, of May 1st, said that $500 was immediately subscribed. The sum needed was obtained, and Nalle returned to Troy a free man.

New Albany, Indiana. Marshal Akers went on board several steamers to search for an alleged fugitive. On board the *Baltic*, he found a man named Tom Bishop, whom he arrested as the slave of a Mr. Miller, living about five miles from Louisville, Ky. He is said to have acknowledged himself a slave, and to have declared his determination to runaway again. He was taken to Kentucky without any " disturbance." — *New Albany Ledger*, April 30, 1860.

Aurora, Illinois. Two colored men at this place were arrested by officers, without warrant or papers of any kind, and on the bare suspicion that they were fugitives from slavery, in the hope that a reward would be offered. " They were taken to Lawrenceburg, to be placed in the county jail, but the jail officers refused to recognize the authority of the captors. They were then carried back to Aurora, and there threatened and abused until the indignation of the community against the men who had arrested them began to be expressed in such unmistakeable terms that they let their prisoners go. The latter had not passed the corporation limits, however, before they were pursued by a rowdy mob, against whom they bravely defended themselves, levelling a number of their assailants to the ground. Being at last overcome, they were bound with cords, and horribly beaten with brass knuckles. Soon after, their master (a Baptist preacher of Boone County, Kentucky) arrived, but was so shocked at the treatment his men had received, that he refused to give any reward to their captors, and said " he had much rather the runaways

had gone to Canada than received such inhuman abuse." —
Cincinnati Commercial, May 10, 1860.

Audacious Attempt to Kidnap a Free Man. "A bold
attempt to kidnap a free negro and carry him across the river
for the purpose of selling him into servitude was made yesterday afternoon, at the river landing, but very fortunately the
ruse of the miscreant who made the effort proved unsuccessful.

"The name of the man is Jeremiah Johnson, and of the negro, James Upson. Johnson met Upson at the landing, and
asked him if he wished a situation on the river. Upson said
that he did, and accompanied Johnson to the Walnut street
ferry landing. Johnson then said that the ferry-boat was the
craft that wished to engage a hand; but the negro, too wide
awake to trust his person upon that boat, demurred to going on
board, at which Johnson seized him by the neck, and, pointing a revolver in his face, told him that if he made the slightest resistance, or refused to board the boat, he would blow his
brains out. This gentle admonition to the negro, who hesita-
ted not a second between liberty and death, was, however,
disregarded, and, shrieking at the top of his voice, he soon gathered about him a large crowd. Johnson affirmed to the
crowd that the negro was a fugitive, and offered twenty dollars to any one who would help to place him on the ferry-
boat and secure his transit across the river. The negro, during all this, was begging piteously to be rescued, and stated that
he was not a fugitive, nor had he ever been a slave. At this
juncture, two gentlemen passed along the levee in a carriage,
one of whom shouted to Johnson to let the negro go, whereupon Johnson called them d—d abolitionists, with other insulting language. The gentleman to whom Johnson's words
were especially directed immediately jumped from the carriage, and, seizing the would-be kidnapper by the hair, pulled
him to the ground, and administered a severe beating. Officers Colby, Chumley and Brockington here arrived, and, re-
leasing Johnson from the fury of the insulted gentleman, conveyed him to the Hammond street station-house. The negro
Upson is well known in this city.

"Against Johnson there seems to be the most positive case.
He will be taken before the Police Court this morning for
preliminary examination."— *Cincinnati Gazette*, May 29.

Slave-Hunter Attacked by Negroes. "On Monday night last, the usually quiet borough of Blairsville, Pennsylvania, was the scene of a disgraceful riot, caused by the appearance of a Virginian in that place, in search of fugitive slaves. It appears that six slaves had left their masters in Hampshire County, Virginia, two of whom had first broken open the store of their master, and helped themselves to some ready-made clothing; two others had each stolen a good rifle-gun, and one of these had helped himself to a suit of his master's clothes. R. H. Patterson, of Springfield, Va., who has been constable for a number of years, together with another person whose name is not given, were despatched after the fugitives, and traced them to a point near Johnstown, in Cambria County. Mr. Patterson received a despatch from Ebensburgh, stating that the fugitives had made their way to Blairsville, and he arrived there on Monday, stopped at the Market House, and made such exploration about town as satisfied him that the fugitives were not in that place, and intended leaving for Johnstown on Tuesday morning. On Monday night, near 10 o'clock, on coming down street to his hotel, in company with another person, and when not far distant from it, he was attacked by a band of negroes, who asked him a question or two about his business, but almost instantly knocked him down. He escaped with his life with great difficulty."

JAMES WAGGONER, *a Free Man, sold as a Slave.* "About six months ago, a colored man named Waggoner was carried across the river from Cincinnati, and found his way into the Newport (Ky.) jail, as a fugitive from labor. About the same time, two men were arrested and committed to the same jail upon the charge of kidnapping Waggoner. When these men were brought up for trial, no one appeared against them, and they were discharged. Waggoner remained in jail, however. No one claimed his service, but the law requires that he shall prove his freedom. This he has not done, and hence he is to be sold on Monday next to the highest bidder. If a man commits murder, or is arrested upon the charge of murder, the State is required to prove him guilty, failing in which, the prisoner is set at liberty; but if a negro is charged with the crime of being a slave, he is required to prove that he is a freeman, failing in which, he is sold at auction and con-

signed to slavery for life! Waggoner, it appears, has worked
in this city. His parents reside in Bantam, Clermont County,
Ohio. They have visited him, and recognized him as their
son. But, being black, their testimony is worthless in a
slave State. To prevent the sale, the right of Waggoner to
freedom must be established by the evidence of white citizens;
and, even then, it will require two or three hundred dollars
to get him out of the net that the avaricious officials of Kentucky have thrown around him. It is hardly possible that
the citizens of Kentucky will countenance this impending
outrage; but, however this may be, the friends of humanity
should see that Waggoner does not lose his freedom, if two or
three hundred dollars will save him from the auction-block."

The Consummation. "James Waggoner has been sold into
slavery, with what attendant circumstances of disregard to
law, unfairness and cheating generally, a full account in our
local columns will show. If any one of our readers can read
that account and be unmoved to anger and detestation, he
possesses a temperament which nothing could excite. Here
is a free man, a man born of parents legally freed and residing as free in Ohio, kidnapped, kept in jail six months, and
finally sold for jail fees, while his kidnappers were allowed to
escape. Of the disgraceful alacrity to enslave a human being, which certain individuals in Newport have manifested, we
cannot trust ourselves to speak.

"Not only has a grievous and irreparable wrong been done
to Waggoner, but the honor of the great State of Kentucky,
in whose name the wrong was committed, has been sullied,
and the dignity of the State of Ohio insulted; for an Ohio-
an has been made a slave by tricks which would disgrace a
'shyster' before the lowest of human tribunals, the Toombs
Police Court in New York."—*Cincinnati Gazette.*

Fuller particulars may be found in the *Standard*, June 23,
1860. On his trial before the Newport Mayor, although the
evidence of his being a free man was of the strongest character, he was declared to be a slave. He was immediately hurried off to a neighboring town and sold to Dr. J. Q. A. Foster,
of Newport, for $700, on his note, with an endorser, said to
be irresponsible. Waggoner was sent to Lexington, Ky., and
placed for sale in the "negro-pens of that city."

Efforts were made to save Waggoner from the terrible pit

into which he had fallen; and not without success, though the obstacles were neither few nor small. His suit for freedom came up before the Circuit Court in Newport, Ky., on the 15th, and it was clearly established that the alleged fugitive was born in 1840, in Brown County, Ohio, of free parents. The Court took time to consider its decision whether the free citizen of that State shall be again permitted to enjoy the liberty slavery has for nearly a year defrauded him of.

Later. "The Kentucky Court declared James Waggoner a free man—free to go where he pleased. Yet only two months since, he was sold in Kentucky on the auction-block as a slave! How is he to obtain justice for the wrongs done to him by the accursed institution of human slavery ?"—*Cleveland Leader*, August, 1860.

Kidnapping at Washington, Fayette County, Ohio, June 27, 1860. A negro man, named JOHN MARSHALL, was kidnapped from this place by three "gentlemen" who came by the midnight train from Cincinnati; they seized the negro early in the morning, and bore him away by railroad, without calling on any officers or authorities of the place. Marshall had lived five years in Washington, and, though once a slave, had been emancipated, and then removed to Brown County, Ohio. He was about 28 years of age. In August, says the *Cincinnati Commercial*, river Policemen Colby and Chumley arrested two brothers named James and Thomas Heise, on a charge of being concerned in the abduction of Marshall.

New York Citizen carried into Slavery. GEORGE ARMSTRONG, a free colored man, born in Jefferson County, New York, left that neighborhood about three weeks since, in the employ of a man named Benjamin. Nothing more was heard from George, until his sister received a letter, on the 5th inst., from Carusi & Miller, lawyers of Washington city, saying that George was in jail there as a fugitive slave. Governor Morgan at once despatched an agent to Washington, with authority to act in the case. — *Albany Evening Journal*, July 7, 1860.

Man Kidnapped in Southern Illinois. "An advertisement in the Jonesboro' *Gazette* brings to our notice the last kidnapping case in Egypt. It announces that a colored man,

'weighing 190 pounds,' is in the custody of the *postmaster*
of Dongola, Union County, Ill. The said negro is embellish-
ed with cuts which may have been made with a knife or whip,
and several gunshot wounds adorn his person — the latest one
having been inflicted by his captor, the postmaster aforesaid!
The advertisement states that he was apprehended by Mr.
Postmaster and carried to Cape Girardeau, Missouri, for the
purpose of finding his ' owner,' but no person appearing to
claim him, he was brought back to Dongola. While on the
way to the latter place, he attempted to escape from his captor, but was brought to by the prompt use of a *shot gun !* " —
Chicago Press and Tribune, July 19.

More Illinois Freemen Kidnapped at Clifton. So interesting is the account which follows, and so remarkable and
so fortunate the experience of one of the victims, that it is
given unabridged, notwithstanding its length. The slaveholder's heart shall yet be reached, and the last may yet be
among the first.

Southern Illinois has been for a long time the hunting-
ground of the men-stealers, and it is stated that within the
past ten years, scores, perhaps hundreds, of freemen have
been kidnapped. The law is powerless to punish the villains,
or to bring the captives back. There are dozens of counties
in which no man of color is safe, and there are men who live
by making negroes their prey. The *Chicago Tribune* says
" there is hope in the future," and gives the following interesting account of the recent kidnapping case at Clifton, Illinois.

On Sunday, June 3d, 1860, three colored men, living in or
near Clifton — a village near Ashkum, a station on the Illinois Central road about sixty miles from Chicago — were enticed by seven or eight whites into a country store or grocery,
and when there, were pounced upon by their armed decoys,
now turned assailants, and under threats of instant death
from revolvers pointed at their breasts, were compelled to
submit to the commands of those who by force and fraud had
overpowered them. They were instantly hurried off to Ashkum, and their captors, having timed their movements to cor-
respond with the motions of the down train, thrust their prey,
still guarded by an array of pistols and bowie knives, into
the cars, and bore the poor men off. All this was accom-

plished without a process of any sort — by brute force alone, illegally and diabolically. The indignation of the quiet community in which this occurred was thoroughly aroused by the outrage; but all parties — the wronged and the wrong doers — were gone — hid in a slave State, under the shadow of the institution that justifies all such atrocities, and everybody despaired of being able to bring the captives back, or the scoundrels to the punishment that they had richly earned.

The kidnapped men were carried to St. Louis as fast as steam could convey them, jealously guarded all the way. Arrived there, they were thrust into a negro-pen, which still disgraces that free soil city, and the work, with a view to the profits of the great crime, was commenced. In answer to the inquiry directed to each, "Who is your master?" one averred that he was then, and always had been, a free man; another refused to answer; while the third, the man Jim, said that he had been the property of Aime Pernard, a farmer near Carondelet, seven miles from the city. The man who claimed to be free and his silent fellow-prisoner were tied up and cruelly flogged, the one to refresh his recollection of the servitude that his captors suspected, and the other to open his mouth to a confession which he would not make. Whipping proving of no avail, other forms of cruelty, hunger the most potent, were tried, but with no better success. At last, both of these men — one torn ruthlessly from his wife and children, and the other from a neighborhood in which his industry had made him respected, and each from a life of freedom and enjoyment — were sent South and sold. They were prisoners of war, and as such, in this time of peace, were compelled to submit to the captors' will. In a State which permits the buying and selling of men and women, and accounts it patriotism, what could they do? Poor, friendless, and black, adjudged to have no rights that white men are bound to respect, what could they do? The tide that has overwhelmed four millions of their kind has overborne them. They sunk into the great vortex, never to be heard of more. A "nigger funeral" — perchance of some unfortunate creature who has died under the lash for his repeated attempts to regain freedom, or of one whom a rifle shot sent into the swamp had killed, or of a man prematurely worn out by labor, and the whip, hunger, and the branding iron — will close

the earthly career of each. There is a hereafter. "Blessed
are the poor in spirit, for theirs is the kingdom of heaven;
blessed are they that mourn, for they shall be comforted!"

While this whipping, shipping and selling was going on,
Aime Pernard, the owner of Jim, was visited by one of the
kidnappers. He went with offers to buy Jim, running — buy
the chances of a capture, after five years of absence. One
hundred dollars was the sum named for this fugitive piece of
flesh and blood. But it was indignantly refused. The sum
was doubled, trebled, quadrupled, and at last multiplied by
ten; but all temptations failed to get them a legal title to
their prey. They served this purpose, however. The owner's
suspicions were aroused by the amount offered by the scoundrels, and their unconcealed eagerness to effect a trade. On
Saturday, a week after the capture, he sent a negro woman
into St. Louis — the woman being the mother of Jim — to
make the inquiries that the case seemed to demand. Her
mother's instinct led her to the right place. Admitted to the
pen, she recognized her son, learned from his lips his suffering and danger; and then with such speed as she could command, hurried back to the master's house. Her story sent
him into the city and to the slave-pen direct. Jim's story
was repeated with such emphasis and particularity that every
drop of that master's blood tingled in his veins. His hag-
gard appearance, his wound and marks of stripes, attested to
the master's sight the truth of the words that fell upon his
ears. He called the keeper of the place, commanded the humane treatment of his charge, and left with the promise he
would return and relieve him of his charge. This was on
Sunday morning. Bright and early on the day following,
Aime Pernard appeared again at the prison gate. To pay
the sum ($100) allowed by the law of the State to the cap-
tors of a fugitive, the jail fees, amounting to $35 more, and
to rig Jim out in a new suit which his master had brought
along, was but a half hour's work. When done, the two
went back to Carondelet, Jim yet doubtful of his fate. But
after a day or two, his case was talked over between his master and himself; and when we state the result, we afford
proof of Jim's eloquence and the generosity and nobleness of
the master's heart. Jim's free papers were made out, his
stock of money was considerably increased, a ticket to Clifton

was put in his hand, and walking by the side of his late master, now protector and friend, the two crossed the Mississippi into Illinois. Here, seating him in the Northern train, the master, with tears flowing down his cheeks and a warm pressure of the hand, bade Jim good bye, and invoked for him God's blessing to speed him on the way!

On Wednesday evening, Jim made his appearance suddenly and without warning at Clifton, whence he had been carried off. He was waving his free paper over his head. A little crowd collected around him, and he briefly related his adventures, and the kindness of that master. A gentleman harnessed a horse to take him to the farm where he had been employed, and another, with rare consideration, rode off to warn Jim's wife of his return and coming. "Niggers have no feeling; it don't hurt 'em to have their domestic life made the plaything of white men's cupidity and lust," say the man-sellers. That strong woman's cry of joy as she clasped her husband in her arms; her devout thanksgiving to God that her life was not left all dark; her breaking down under the flood of emotion which the glad event aroused; her sobs and plaints, interrupted only by unuttered prayers to the Father of white and black alike; the deep feeling Jim displayed; that delicious joy ennobled by the new consciousness of freedom and security in the possession of a wife and home, — these, leaving not a dry eye in that little crowd of lookers-on, disprove the slander. And to-day, the relation of the scene at that meeting, even in Clifton, where it is a thrice-told tale, brings tears from eyes that are unused to weep.

There is not much to add to this narrative. The ladies of Clifton, moved by the rare generosity of Aime Pernard, united in a letter thanking him in warm terms for what he had done, and inviting him to pay them a visit at his earliest convenience, that they might in person point out to him the evidence of the good he had done.

Mr. Pernard's reply to the ladies was a very honorable and noble one, which, but for its length, would have been inserted here.

High-handed Outrage on a Free Man in Philadelphia. The following is taken from the Philadelphia *North American* of Monday, July 30, 1860 : —

"On Friday afternoon last, three men arrived in this city

from Georgetown, D. C. They exhibited a power of attorney to the U. S. Marshal, and announced that they were authorized to undertake the rendition to servitude of one Ben Hurd, a slave who had escaped to Philadelphia from one Joshua Bateman, of Georgetown, his lawful owner.

" A warrant was obtained from Judge Cadwallader for the capture of the alleged runaway, and on Saturday morning, Deputy Marshals Sharkey and Jenkins, in company with the three negro-hunters, started in pursuit of the concealed fugitive. Supposing, very naturally, that the runaway had obtained employment as a waiter in one of the hotels, they started upon a tour of discovery among the various hotels. They had almost given up the search, when, between 8 and 9 A. M. on Saturday, in passing up Fifth street, near Market, a stalwart colored man, driving a dray towards them, burst upon their delighted view. A shout of exultation went up from the Georgetown men, as they hastily examined the negro. 'That's the rascal!' said one. 'The very nigger!' exclaimed the other. 'Catch the runaway, Mr. Marshal!' cried the third; and without another word, Messrs. Sharkey and Jenkins seized the horse by the head. The 'nigger' was taken by the leg and the coat collar, and lifted off his dray in a very decided hurry. His wrists were then placed in nippers, and, long before the poor fellow precisely understood what all the proceedings meant, he was hustled into the Marshal's office, at Fifth and Chestnut streets.

A crowd collected, and not a few persons, commiserating the condition of the black man, as they looked at his pinioned hands and rent garments, wanted to know upon what charge the arrest was made, and what was meant by the whole business. The prisoner very naturally united in the request, and demanded to know why he had been assaulted and imprisoned. At this juncture, several citizens came voluntarily forward and informed the officers that they had made a mistake; that the man in their custody, so far from being a fugitive from labor, had been a resident of Philadelphia for many years. When confronted with the outraged man, the Georgetown men were obliged to yield their point, and with shamed faces acknowledged that the present prisoner WAS NOT THEIR MAN!!

" Of course, after this, the prisoner was discharged. His

name is James Valentine, who came from a free parentage in Salem, N. J., is now fifty years of age, and has lived in this city since 1826. He has driven a dray for the last twenty-six years, has made some property, and resides in his own house in Whitehall street. We understand that Valentine will bring a suit against the Marshals for the assault upon him — a suit whose burden has been thrown upon the Marshals, the Georgetowners having shaken the dust from their shoes and vacated the city. The Simon-pure Ben Hurd by this time has probably started for Canada, and the representatives of Mr. Bateman may as well give up his capture as a bad job."

On the foregoing case, the Philadelphia correspondent of the *Anti-Slavery Standard* thus remarks :

" It was another *Adam Gibson* case. The bloodhounds of the law mistook their man. Happily, the slave-master was not entirely devoid of honesty ; otherwise, the poor fellow might to-day be in the pen of a Southern slave-trader.

" This circumstance illustrates anew the atrocity of the Fugitive Slave Bill. No man is safe under its operation. Our most respectable citizens, if their skins be dark, are liable, like James Valentine, to be seized, manacled, and dragged before heartless officials, with little hope of deliverance, except it be found in the tender mercies of the slaveholder. For since *Judge* Cadwallader has taken the place of *Commissioner* Ingraham, and Jenkins and Sharkey have undertaken to do the work of George Alberti, the captured black man has but little to hope for from our Philadelphia officials.

" We had hoped that our city had seen an end to slave-catching, but since the accession of Cadwallader to the bench, and owing, perhaps, to the ease with which a slave-warrant may now be obtained, the infamous business seems to have acquired a new lease of existence.

" Steps have been taken to bring the perpetrators of this outrage to justice, which I trust will prove successful. They should be prosecuted to the uttermost." — *Standard*, August 4, 1860.

Stealing Free Negroes in Maryland, &c. This barbarism of slavery appears to be carried on quite extensively by Virginia dealers in human flesh about Alexandria. We learn by

7

the *Baltimore Clipper* that recently ten free negroes, seven
men, and three women, were unlawfully abducted from the
State of Maryland and taken to Alexandria. Five of the
men and three women were sold to go South, and being helpless and friendless, were carried off into life servitude. The
Mayor of Alexandria, hearing of the outrage, sent a detective to the negro jails of the city, and found two of the abducted men, who had been left at the establishment of Price,
Burch & Co., for safe keeping. Proceedings were instituted,
and the two free men were returned to Baltimore. Of course,
the kidnappers go free of proper punishment in Virginia. —
Cleveland Leader, August, 1860.

Virginia Law, Chivalry, and Dignity! The following
illustrates too clearly the kidnapping and man-stealing spirit
engendered by the Fugitive Slave Law to be omitted here :

Over Eleven Hundred Free Negroes for Sale. " On
Thursday, in front of the Court House, eleven hundred and
ninety-three free negroes will be offered for sale, for a sufficient time to enable them by their allowance per diem to pay
their taxes. Some of these negroes are indebted as much as
$25 to the city, and as they generally sell for ten cents a day,
their value will no doubt be made out of them. All of them
are lazy rascals, showing conclusively that their freedom is a
drawback upon them, and proving how worthless is the race,
if unguided by the hand of the white man. The sale is to
commence at ten o'clock."—*Petersburg (Va.) Express.*

The Petersburg (Va.) Free Negro Sale. The Petersburg
Express says : — " The decisive measures of the officers of the
tax regime brought all free negrodom up standing. Out of
the entire number who were to be sold for their taxes, only
one hundred and forty-nine were disposed of ; three hundred
and fifty came forward and paid their taxes, and the rest found
no purchasers. The sales varied from ten to twenty-five cents
per diem, the purchaser to own the negro until his wages, at
such rates, should pay his delinquent taxes, and thus free him
from bondage. There were many who came to pay up at the
eleventh hour, who were sold to themselves at as high as one
dollar a day."

More Virginia Chivalry, with a Clerical Sample! Some
five years ago, Mr. Duval, of Chesterfield, missed one of his

likeliest negro men, and though repeated endeavors were made to discover his whereabouts, he still remained at large. A few days ago, Mr. Duval learned that he would probably capture the runaway by a strict alert in or about Richmond, and pursuing this course, with the assistance of some of the Richmond police, he succeeded. Yesterday morning, when he was about to take him from that city, and had arrived at the Petersburg depot, the negro broke away and fought with terrific fury against his master and the police officers who accompanied him. He was finally subdued, handcuffed and safely placed on board the train. At the half-way station, Mr. Duval left the cars with his negro, and placing him in a buggy, drove towards home. They had not proceeded far before the negro succeeded in getting one of the handcuffs off, and assailed his master with desperation, evidently with the intention to kill or seriously injure him. But Mr. Duval being a resolute man, of firm calibre, and a quick eye, met the assault, and for upwards of half an hour the master and slave scuffled and fought in the buggy. They proceeded thus for about half a mile, the fight growing more fearful as they continued, when they were met by the Rev. Charles T. Friend. This circumstance was fortunate for Duval, who would no doubt have been finally overpowered. He called to Mr. Friend to assist him. In a short time, the negro was overpowered and tied firmly with ropes and spare reins; but the giant strength of the refractory slave had rather increased than diminished, and he snapped the ropes that were twisted about his arms like so much twine, and again offered a fearful resistance. They were now without any other immediate means of securing him, although they quickly succeeded in overpowering him. Fortunately, Mrs. Friend, who witnessed the scene with firmness and without fear, having in her carriage fifteen yards of cotton cloth, which she had purchased, suggested that that would answer for a rope, and at once producing it, folded it, with her husband's aid, to sufficient size for the purpose, and with it the negro was tied beyond all possibility of escape. He was then taken safely home. Both Mr. Duval's and the negro's clothing was almost completely stripped from them, such had been the fight. — *Petersburg (Va.) Express*, August, 1860.

A pretty business for a Reverend and a Reverend's wife to

engage in, says the *Anti-Slavery Bugle* of August 25. A professed ambassador of Christ catching negroes! A woman tying up fugitive slaves!

Kidnapping on a Large Scale in Kansas. So long as the Fugitive Slave Law exists, practices and deeds of darkness like the following (the account of which, though requiring space to record, must not be omitted) will continue both to abound and to increase. Into what a depth of heathenism and barbarity has the nation sunk! " For cold-blooded atrocity and diabolical cruelty," says the Lawrence (K.) *Republican*, " the cases here narrated by a reliable correspondent at Wyandot stand preëminent."

WYANDOT, K. T., August 4, 1860.

EDITOR REPUBLICAN :

DEAR SIR, — A deep sense of duty impels me to make a few suggestions, and give some information, touching the present condition of our Territory — especially the Missouri border — relative to a class of human beings, created in God's own image, who are so unfortunate as to be even suspected of being of African descent.

Within the last few weeks, our county has been made the theatre for the transaction of some of the boldest, most revolting and tragic scenes that have ever occurred in our midst — the principal actors in which are men living in our own midst, some of them holding both United States and Territorial offices. Not long since, a man by the name of Hope, with scarcely a drop of African blood running in his veins, and never a slave, was most brutally kidnapped, in open day, from Joe Armstrong's — a Delaware Indian, living just on the edge of the prairie, about twelve miles west of our city. Poor Hope was lashed to a horse and hurried to the Kaw bottoms, whipped until his back was one mass of gore, and when night came, was hurried off to Missouri, and finally wound up in the St. Joseph jail, and soon was sold for twelve hundred dollars to a " Southern trader," destined to perpetual bondage. This same Hope was kidnapped two years ago, and placed in the jail at Independence, from whence he was taken by a writ of *habeas corpus*, through the exertions of Judge Wright — since which time, the St. Joseph jail has become the slave mart for the use of all the devils incarnate that desire to rob, murder, kidnap or steal.

A few weeks since, two negroes were decoyed from a German boarding-house in Wyandot, by false pretences, and taken to Kansas City — the perpetrators stating on their return that they were slaves, and that their masters gave them two hundred and fifty dollars for their recovery. It turns out, however, that these two men were never slaves, but that just before reaching Kansas City, they were inhumanly whipped, to make them state who were their owners, which they failed to do — the negroes choosing to die under the torturing strap, rather than own to a *lie*. (I may as well state here, lest I forget it, that the method pursued by all these *fiends of hell* in the shape of kidnappers, is to whip their unfortunate victims on their bare backs, while their hands and feet are heavily loaded down with irons, and their mouths gagged, until they acknowledge that they are slaves, and state who were their masters — no matter who — some name must be selected. There are very few who can refrain, while under this exquisite torture, and when a horrible death seems certain at the hands of their hardened tormentors, from speaking some name. After this, the weak and bleeding victim is hurried off to Missouri — first to the *St. Jo. jail*, thence by "traders" to the blackness and darkness of Southern bondage.) From the Kaw bottoms, where these men were whipped, they were taken to their pretended master in Kansas City, who turned out to be the notorious Jake Hurd. Thence they were taken to the St. Joseph jail, where, ten days ago, Jake Hurd was still trying to sell them into Southern slavery ; and unless ere this some *Doy rescuers* have liberated them, they have gone to the dank, lone rice swamps of the South.

On the 18th of July, a man by the name of C. W. Jones — with straight hair, not having a drop of African blood in him, and never a slave, his ancestors having been all white, excepting one of his great grandfathers, four generations back, who came from and was a native of the island of Madagascar, but on arriving in this country, married a white English woman — this man Jones was living with his mother, sister, brother, and two of his own little light-haired girls, at Charles Armstrong's (a Delaware Indian living near Joe Armstrong's, spoken of above). They had taken some land to cultivate, and were gaining an honest living in peace and contentment. Late in the evening of the 18th ult., four men stopped at Armstrong's for the night. Armstrong was gone. About midnight, these men desired to leave. Jones assisted them in preparing their horses and wagon, and just as he was turning to ask Mrs. Armstrong the amount of their bill, he was seized, choked, gagged and pounded until he was senseless, from which condition he awoke, finding himself in the laps of two of his captors, driving with all speed on the open prairie, in the two-horse wagon, while the other two rode on horseback. The first sounds he heard were the voices of these wretches bewailing their loss, fearing that their booty was dead. He also found himself secured with heavy iron handcuffs. To be brief, this Jones was taken that night to within two miles of this place, into the Kaw bottoms, to an empty log cabin. The next morning, a young Indian, passing with his gun in pursuit of squirrels, found *Samuel Forsyth*, Ex-Sheriff of Wyandot County, now Deputy U. S. Marshal, and one of the County Commissioners of this county, watching at the door of the cabin, and poor Jones, manacled and sore, prostrate within. Soon, Louis M. Cox, a resident of this place, appears. They state to the young Indian that " the nigger " was a horse thief, and that they caught him stealing Lowe's horse; and after exciting the Indian's sympathies against the pretended thief, they hire him for a dollar to watch him, while they go away. They now take Jones away further into the deep, lone woods, into a dark ravine, beneath a fallen tree, where no human eye could find him, and there chain him with a heavy chain and lock to a tree — leaving directions to blow his brains out, if he moves or speaks. Honest Indian, never suspecting wrong, obeys with all fidelity. About noon, his captors return with two fresh recruits, who take him away, saying they are going to Leavenworth to try him; and the Indian goes home, being told never to say a word about the matter. The nigger-stealers hurry poor Jones into a still deeper and darker solitude, where they lay bare his back, and tell him that they will whip him " to death, unless he owns up to having a master." They lay Jones upon his face on the ground, and with a pistol belt whip and beat him until they are exhausted themselves; then rest, and whip him again — but no master's name comes from the lips of the helpless mass of living gore before them. With curses they now stoop to feel his pulse, and ask who owned his father? Jones in feeble tones answers, " My father was always free." Again the dripping scourge falls upon the quivering flesh. " Who, now, owned your father, you d——d lying nigger? Who was his father ? " With a broken voice, expecting soon to die, poor Jones whispers, " Drury Jennins was my father's father." (Drury Jennins, a white man of Tennessee, was Jones's grandfather, and never a slave.) Tired with their exercise, they now cover the clotted back with the poor man's clothes, and wait for darkness to hide them from the eye of man, (but the Eye that slumbereth not, nor sleepeth, was watching them). As soon as it was safe, the party proceeded down through Wyandot, to just above the Kansas ferry — avoiding all the public streets — where they set across the Kansas river, and thence on to Kansas City, Mo. — Jones being bareheaded all this time, save going through this city, when Cox lent him his hat, for fear some one would meet them and notice poor Jones's head, which had been closely sheared. From Kansas City, Jones was taken by one of the party in a two-horse buggy to the *jail in St. Joseph.* Here Jones found Jake Hurd and kindred spirits. He remained in jail several days, being daily examined by traders, to whom he told his story, and constantly inquired for pen, ink and paper, showing that he was educated. The traders, after examining him, would exclaim that they "*wanted a little nigger blood in the slaves they bought!*" In a few days, it becoming evident that no money could be made out of Jones, Messrs. Cox and Forsyth, who had been hanging around St. Joseph for a day or two, made their appearance before Jones, telling him they were *mistaken in their man,* and that he could go, desiring to take him back. Jones, however, preferred being his own conductor, fearing that foul play was intended, inasmuch as he was *strongly advised by them that it would be much better for him not to go back into the Territory.* Jones, however, managed to arrive in a few days in Quindaro, and soon made an affidavit which brought Messrs. Cox and Forsyth before Justices Chadwick and Duncan, of Quindaro, where proof as positive as Holy Writ was shown against said Forsyth and Cox — showing that from first to last they were the prime movers in this diabolical outrage. After hearing the evidence of Jones, Gen. A. C. Davis, counsel for defence, for his clients waived any further examination, and gave bonds for their appearance before the next District Court.

But the scene does not close here. Poor Jones must not be left to tell his story to the world. Immediately after the Court adjourned, Mr. Davis swore out a writ against Jones, stating that about the 18th of July, said Jones passed counterfeit money; and Jones is hurried off to Wyandot, to wait an examination before P. S. Post, acting as U. S. Commissioner. On the next day, at the hour for trial, half a dozen of our best lawyers appeared as counsel for the prisoner; but no witnesses could be found for the prosecution. Something must be done, else Jones would again be at large, and tell of his wrongs. Mr. Attorney-General Davis makes an affidavit for a continuance, on the ground that one James Lester, to whom said Jones gave a counterfeit gold dollar, was in Missouri, and other evidence was absent. A continuance was granted until this date, and Mr. Jones was let out on one hundred dollars bail. At the appointed hour, three witnesses made their appearance, and were duly sworn, to wit. Louis M. Cox, James Lester, and Cornelius Sager. The moment James Lester and Cornelius Sager were seen by Mr. Jones, they were recognized as being the men who assisted Cox and Forsyth when he was cruelly whipped, and Lester as the man who took him in a buggy from Kansas City to the St. Joseph jail. These were the men that Gen. Davis had for witnesses, to swear poor Jones into criminal bondage — the same men having failed to kidnap him into the bondage of slavery. Cox and Lester swore positively to taking a counterfeit two-dollar-and-a-half gold piece and two counterfeit half-dollar pieces from Jones on the 19th of July; but on cross-examination, swore that this was done while Jones was their prisoner, handcuffed, and away alone near the log cabin in the Kaw bottoms. Sager took alarm, and left secretly before his turn for swearing came. Immediately after Lester had told his story, he ran to the Kansas river, sprang into a boat evidently prepared for him, and kept loose by a little boy, and shoved out into the stream. Officer Sawyer, who had writs for both Lester and Sager, for kidnapping Jones, was in close pursuit, but supposed Lester was going to the ferry, and thus lost sight of him until he (Lester) was well under way. Taking another boat, with three men, he however commenced the chase. Sawyer rapidly gained upon the brigand thief, and when nearly half a mile down the Missouri river — into which Lester had rowed, hoping to gain the Missouri State line — the officer's boat came within a few feet of the kidnapper's. At this time, the brigand, being heavily armed, threatened to blow out the brains of the man that pulled the next oar. The man at the oars — there being but one pair — instantly dropped them, and fled to the back part of the boat, and no power could induce either of his two companions to raise a finger in further pursuit. The brave Sawyer, whose mettle has been tried before, and never fails, sprang to the oar and pulled with all his might and main; but the current was swift, and the boat large and heavily laden, in comparison with Lester's light skiff, and the time lost by the cowardly refusal of the rower to continue his efforts, before the officer could get the boat under way again, was so great that the brigand thief was within the jurisdiction of Kansas City, his Missouri home, before he could be overtaken, and thus was lost. It is to be hoped, however, for her credit as well as safety, that Kansas City will rid herself of the numerous Jake Hurds, Tobe Owens, Jim Lesters, and a large lot more of kindred pimps that now make that city their head-quarters. It is ascertained beyond a doubt that there exists in that city, and in various parts of Kansas Territory, a large and dangerous band of men — many of them holding high positions in community — who are banded together for the purpose of kidnapping free men, and selling them into slavery; of stealing slaves, and selling them still further South; and of keeping them in confinement until a large reward is offered, and then taking them back and obtaining the reward. A portion of them make counterfeiting their business, while still another enrich their purses by stealing horses. No community in Kansas or Missouri is safe from these villains.

Too much credit cannot be given to those of our lawyers who dared to do right, and perform the duty of defending Jones against the last attempt, by fraud and perjury, to place him where he could have no contact with the world, and to throw around an innocent and harmless man the garb of the criminal — thus hoping to blast his character, and relieve others from the dark load of guilt and crime they now carry on their shoulders.

Mr. Post, after listening patiently to the evidence and pleas of counsel, decided very promptly that no evidence of crime had been shown on the part of Mr. Jones, and the prisoner was instantly discharged, to the entire satisfaction of every honest man who heard the evidence, and knew the facts in the case.   Yours, for justice,   *

Minneapolis, Minnesota. Extract of a letter from a friend in Minneapolis (Minnesota), dated Aug. 20th, 1860 :

" One week ago yesterday, a slave was set free in this place. She is still in safe hands, and probably will not be retaken without the shedding of blood. The many slave-holders, and their base and servile panderers, who are here at this time, will, undoubtedly, make an effort to kidnap her, if they can learn her whereabouts. There is great excitement here in regard to the matter, and violence is threatened. A forcible but unsuccessful attempt was made to kidnap the released slave the night after her freedom was decreed." — *Liberator.*

Attempted Kidnapping at Cincinnati, Sept. 1860. A mulatto of Cincinnati, named A. W. Thompson, in company with James Franklin, a blind white man of Columbia, South Carolina, have been arrested at Memphis, Tennessee, for attempting to sell a free negro into bondage. The Memphis *Enquirer* says :

"James Franklin is said to be a man of means, living in Columbia, S. C., and a little fast in his expenditures for a blind man. It is supposed that the wily Cincinnati free negro conceived the idea of selling his dusky-hued brother into slavery, and then inveigled Franklin into it. Fortunately, they are all in jail, and the guilty party will be made to suffer the full penalty of the law."

Fugitive Slave Remanded — Collision between U. S. Officers and the People. Cincinnati, Sept. 23d, 1860. On Thursday last, the U. S. Marshal, with two Deputies and eight or ten men, went to Iberia, Monroe County, in this State, to arrest three slaves, brothers, who ran away from Germantown, Ky., about four months since. One was captured by the Marshal, and after an examination by the Commissioner, Newhall, was remanded to the custody of his former master.

One of the Deputies, in attempting to capture another negro, was set upon by the crowd, who tore off his clothing, and took away his warrant and money, and threatened to hang or shoot him ; but after cropping his hair, they allowed him to depart without the negro. The other Deputy was fired upon while attempting to arrest the third negro, and returning the fire, shot the fingers off the hand of one of the rioters, but was obliged to leave without the negro. — *Boston Transcript*.

Subsequently, the Rev. George Gordon, James Hammond, Ashbury Parker, Calvin Rowland, Joseph T. Baldwin, E. D. Ashbury, and Jonathan McLarew, were indicted by the Grand Jury of the United States Circuit Court of Northern Ohio, for obstructing the United States Marshal and his Deputies, at Iberia, Monroe County, on the 20th of September last, in their efforts to secure, by legal process, a fugitive slave. The same parties are also indicted for assaulting the owners of the negro and their assistants, with a view to prevent the reclamation of the slave, under the Fugitive Slave Law.

United States Marshal Johnson, assisted by Deputies White and Given, spent two days in and about Iberia, in searching for persons indicted by the Grand Jury of the United States Court, as the rescuers in the above case. They arrested three persons, — Archibald Brownlee, Robert McLaren, and Hiram Dunn. Rev. George Gordon, who also had been indicted, had been compelled to flee, it was said, to Canada. Messrs. Brownlee and McLaren gave bonds, in $2000 each, to appear at the March term (1861) of the Court. Mr. Dunn was incarcerated in Cleveland jail. The Cleveland *National Democrat* (!) exults in the arrest of these men, as of persons who had committed some aggravated wickedness.

Kidnapping Free Persons in Galena, Illinois. Another case of kidnapping has occurred in Illinois. On the 28th ultimo, a person representing himself as the agent of parties in Canada, went to Galena to hire men and women to work on a farm and in a hotel in Southern Iowa, expressing his preference for colored persons. He succeeded in engaging Johnny Boyd, a free mulatto, his wife, a colored girl fourteen years old, and the party took with them a small white

child two or three years old. Boyd was subsequently found
murdered, his body lying by the road-side. The circumstances attending his departure from Galena leave no other belief
than that he was enticed away with the intention of enslaving him, and that, becoming suspicious of the intentions of
his employer, he was put to death to make sure of the others
of the party. The citizens have offered a reward of $500 for
the apprehension of the kidnapper and murderer.

A Slave Remanded to his Master. Ex parte application
of David Gibbs in the matter of a *habeas corpus* issued to
try the question of freedom of the boy Henson, about twelve
years of age, and alleged to be illegally deprived of his liberty.

Lewis Bruce, in answer to the writ, stated that he was the
owner of the boy, and was taking him from Virginia, his
former residence, to Missouri; that the boat on which he was
travelling had stopped at Cincinnati Landing, and tied up to
the shore against his wishes.

Jolliffe argued the case for applicant, claiming that the
boy was found within our jurisdiction, and, as slavery could
not exist in Ohio under her Constitution and laws, he must
be declared free.

Judge Gholson (elected last year by the Republicans) announced the decision, (the other members of the Court, Judges Carter, Mallon and Collins, concurring,) and held that although the jurisdiction of our Courts extended for many purposes to boats on the Ohio river, the citizens of Virginia and
other States bordering on the south had a right to the free
navigation of the river ; that the stopping of boats and tying
up at the Landing was a necessary *incident* to the right of
free navigation, and as such rested on a higher basis than the
mere jurisdiction of the river.

In the course of the decision, it was remarked that, while
we should carefully maintain our own rights, yet the Courts
must also see to it that the rights of our neighbors were not
infringed. The Sheriff was directed to return the boy to his
owner on the boat. — *Cincinnati Enquirer*, October, 1860.

Six Negroes Kidnapped near Sandusky. The Sandusky
(Ohio) *Register* of the 15th October, 1860, says that on Friday evening, at about 9 o'clock, two cabins situated on the

"Mills lot," a little south of the Castalia road, about three miles from Sandusky, were surprised by a party of some ten or fifteen kidnappers, and Mr. Marshall and wife, and Mr. Hutchins, wife (a free woman) and two children were taken from their homes, dragged to the railroad, and put on board the night train for Cincinnati, which left Sandusky at ten, P. M. The neighbors were aroused and went to Castalia station to stop the party, but could not find them in the cars. After the cars started, it was discovered that a dark car was attached, and that the kidnappers and their victims had entered that car at Venice siding, near where the assault had been committed. The *Register* says : —

"There were found evidences of pretty severe scuffling about the cabins. Some report that blood was found, and that the course of the party could be traced by blood along the way.

" The children were each about six months old, and were born in Ohio. These persons first came here in December last, as we are told, and some time during the winter rented 30 acres of wild land for five years, put up cabins, and moved on to it in March last. In the spring, they cleared seven acres and put out crops, and the cultivated land is now covered with a fine crop of corn, etc., sufficient for their winter's supply."

The *Cincinnati Gazette* says that the seizure was made by " Deputy United States Marshal Manson and seven aids," — and that the " four fugitive slaves and two free children were all sent, with the help of a U. S. Commissioner, into slavery in Mason County, Ky., whence the four adults had escaped."

Slave-Hunting in Illinois. In Chicago, the other day, a negro woman named Eliza, who had escaped from slavery in the Territory of Nebraska a short time before, was arrested as a fugitive slave. The United States Marshal, in taking the woman to jail, was stopped in the street by an excited crowd, and was compelled to give the woman to the city police, who lodged her in the Armory for safe keeping. The next morning, a Justice issued his warrant against her for a breach of the peace, and she was taken out of the Armory by the Sheriff of the County, and while he was on the way with her to the office of the magistrate, she was rescued by a company of people of her own color and carried off — the wise ones only know whither. The Justice who issued the warrant, the Sheriff who executed it, and seven other persons, have been indicted in the United States District Court for violating the accursed Fugitive Slave Law. Thus is the "irrepressible conflict" kept up! — *Standard*, November 24, 1860.

The *Chicago Tribune* thus speaks of this case : —

"*The Great Case.* The arrest of nine of the alleged rescuers of the negro woman Eliza, who is claimed under the Dred Scot decision as a slave by a citizen of Nebraska, whence she escaped, already excites much interest among the members of the bar in this city. The *Times and Herald*, with indecent haste and upon its own motion, has already tried the case, given the opinion of the Judge, sentenced the prisoners, and restored the serenity of the public mind. We beg our sapient contemporary to observe that its eagerness to impose fines, visit with imprisonment, and settle grave questions of law, is not likely to be gratified. The men under indictment will make a struggle in the Courts, and long before their trials are concluded, the attention of the nation will be devoted to them. That journal will find that the guarantees of freedom in the Territories will not be readily given up.

Gross Act of Kidnapping a Free Man. While the South is clamoring for the repeal of Northern Personal Liberty Laws, the North is constantly reminded, by outrages committed upon unoffending persons within her borders, that the freedom of the citizen cannot be too carefully guarded. A notable case in point is that of the colored man, John Thomas, kidnapped the other day in this city, confined in the United States Grand Jury room, and conveyed to Virginia without any warrant or process whatever! This man, who, by the act of his master in sending him into a free State, is no longer a slave, but a free man, is boldly seized and borne off to slavery. At the last advices, the man was in custody, at Richmond, awaiting the arrival of his late master from Kentucky. This is a case of which Marshal Rynders, District Attorney Roosevelt, and all the United States Commissioners, deny all knowledge. And yet the man was kept a prisoner, without a warrant, in the Grand Jury room of the building which they occupy, and, as we learn, when the *habeas corpus* was applied for in his behalf, was hurried out of the State by one of the Assistant United States Marshals. This act is in flagrant violation of the law of this State. Whether the kidnapped man be free or slave, his abductor has committed a crime punishable by imprisonment in Sing Sing. — *New York Tribune.*

The following is the report of the proceedings on the *habeas corpus* before Judge Mullin :—

" Mr. Vail went to the place designated by John Thomas (the United States Grand Jury room in Chambers street.) It appears that John had contrived to notify Mr. Vail by dropping a note from the window on Reade street, telling a boy where to take it.

" Upon Mr. Vail's arrival, he found John in charge of a person, but whether he was a Marshal's assistant or not is not known. Another person was in the room, and he showed Mr. Vail a power of attorney duly executed in Louisville, and authorizing him to act in behalf of Mr. Winter, the master. John begged his employer to endeavor to purchase him, and, with the hope of gaining time, Mr. Vail consented. A writ of *habeas corpus* was obtained from Judge Ingraham, sitting at the Supreme Court Chambers, and it was served upon Marshal Rynders.

This morning, Nov. 21st, that officer appeared before Judge Mullin, and said that he was ready to make a return to a writ of *habeas corpus* issued to him, and in accordance with its directions, he had brought with him the person named in the writ (pointing to a colored man in the rear of the court-room.)

A young gentleman from Capron & Lake's office appeared as representing the interest of John Thomas. He stated that the return was unsatisfactory, inasmuch as the person produced here was not the one mentioned in the petition — it was a different person altogether.

Marshal Rynders — His name is John Thomas, and he is in my custody.

The counsel replied that the coincidence was extraordinary as well as convenient, but the person sought had not been produced.

Marshal Rynders — I have no other man by that name in my custody.

Judge Mullin — Then, sir, you will have to make a return to that effect.

Marshal Rynders — I have so stated.

Judge Mullin — It is right that the return should be made in writing.

Deputy Marshal Thompson then made the required addition to the return.

The return being satisfactory, the counsel could not press the matter further, and the parties left the court-room.

The day following these proceedings, a despatch from Richmond announced the arrival in that city of the fugitive John Thomas, in the custody of two of Marshal Rynders's deputies. He was put in prison to await the orders of his master at St. Louis. It is said, we presume with truth, that he was carried off without any legal process whatever. Having been sent to a free State by his master, he was not a fugitive from service, according to the provision of the United States Constitution; and if his case had been brought before a Commissioner, and properly argued, he must have been discharged as a free man. It is a clear case of kidnapping, but we doubt very much whether the kidnappers will ever be brought to justice. — *Standard*, Dec. 1, 1860.

Another Kidnapping Attempt in New York. A colored boy named William Percival, 14 years old, recently arrived here in the schooner Napoleon from Trinidad. He says that the captain of the schooner, D. D. Sirmond, (a native of Charleston,) induced him to leave his parents and ship as cabin boy. Learning that the schooner was bound for Charleston, he was afraid of being sold as a slave, and therefore ran away from the boarding-house where the captain had placed him. The captain employed a police officer to hunt him up, but when, after arresting him, the officer heard his story, he called the attention of the Superintendent to the matter, and the boy was finally placed under the care of the British Consul, to be sent to his parents in Trinidad. There is too much reason to believe that Capt. Sirmond meant to consign the boy to a life of slavery. The mate of the schooner told the police officer that William had been indentured to the captain, who had bound himself in $500 to return him; but the captain did not present the indenture, as he would probably have done if he had possessed such a paper. The boy's story is doubtless true, and if so, he has had a narrow escape from a doom worse than death.— *Standard*, Dec. 15, 1860.

Another Fugitive Slave Surrendered. A negro man who had run away from a plantation near Louisville, Tenn., eight months ago, was taken into custody at Cincinnati, a few days since, and delivered to the claimant on showing proof that he was a slave. The *Gazette* of that city remarks: —

"In this case, the anxious politicians of the country may see with what alacrity the Fugitive Slave Law is executed by the citizens of Ohio. This case is a fair illustration of the majority that have occurred during the past three years, as, during this time, not a colored person arrested on a warrant of a United States Commissioner has been set free again or rescued."— *Boston Traveller*, Dec. 29, 1860.

☞ This statement of the *Cincinnati Gazette* might be made, with truth, vastly stronger. In the whole period of ten years since the Fugitive Slave Law was enacted, the number of persons arrested as fugitives, and set free, or rescued, is so insignificant as barely to form a feature in the case; while the number of ACTUALLY FREE persons, STOLEN, KID-NAPPED from the Northern States, and, in utter defiance of law and justice alike, HURRIED INTO SLAVERY, is to be reckoned by hundreds. The slaveholders have ever been the aggressors, the usurpers, the bold and reckless violators of compacts; and have ever practised the policy of calling attention away from past outrage, by inaugurating some new one to throw the former into shadow. The North has been disgracefully, servilely, basely compliant to the Fugitive Slave Law and its iniquitous provisions, and is utterly without excuse for her shame.

Here we close, for the present, the record of the Fugitive Slave Law, as its history has been daily writing itself in our country's annals. Enactment of hell! which has marked every step of its progress over the land by suffering and by crimes,— crimes of the bloodiest dye, sufferings which can never fully be told; which is tracked by the dripping blood of its victims, by their terrors and by their despair; against which, and against that Wicked Nation which enacted it, and which suffers it still to stand as their LAW, the cries of the poor go up continually into the ears of God, — cries of bitterest anguish, mingled with fiercest execrations — thousands of Rachels weeping for their children, and will not be comforted, because they *are not*.

No one can fail to observe how numerous the cases of KIDNAPPING FREE PERSONS become in the latter half of this tract. The number of persons thus seized and carried into slavery, and the brutality and murderous spirit of those engaged in the work, are startling and fearful. The Fugitive Slave Law has built up a regular NORTHERN SLAVE TRADE; and it threatens to victimize every person in whom a suspicion of African blood exists; and it assuredly will not stop with them, as many well authenticated cases already prove.

Judge LEAVITT, of Cincinnati, in his charge to the jury, in the case of Wm. M. Connelly, (May, 1858,) said that " Christian charity was not within the meaning or intent of the Fugitive Slave Law, and it would not, therefore, answer as a defence for violating the law." " This is an admission," says the *New York Independent*, " which shows the infamous nature of that law in a clearer light than any of its enemies have ever depicted it." Does it not also show the counterfeit character of that which extensively passes for piety and Christianity in this country? Judge Leavitt is a member, in good standing, of the Presbyterian Church, and is reputed a very pious man; yet is constantly engaged in enforcing the Fugitive Law, whose character and intent he describes as above.

Reader, is your patriotism of the kind which believes, with the supporters of old despotisms, that the Sovereign Power can do no wrong? Consider the long record which has been laid before you, and say if your country has not enacted a most wicked, cruel and shameful law, which merits only the condemnation and abhorrence of every heart. Consider that this law was aimed at the life, liberty and happiness of the poorest and least-privileged portion of our people — a class whom the laws should befriend, protect, and raise up. What is the true character of a law, whose working, whose fruits are such as this mere outline of its history shows? Is it fit that such deeds and such a law should have your sanction and support? Will you remain in a moment's doubt whether to be a friend or a foe to such a law? Will you countenance or support the man, in the Church or in the State, who is not its open and out-spoken opponent? Will you not, rather, yourself trample it under foot, as alike the disgrace of your country, the foe of humanity, and the foe of God, and nobly join, with heart and hand, every honest man who seeks to load with the opprobrium they deserve, the law itself, and every one that justifies and upholds it?

For, interpret the Constitution as we may, delude ourselves as we please with the idea that because a law is such, it is therefore right and binding on us, we cannot, in conscience or in common sense, escape from the conclusion that the FUGITIVE SLAVE LAW is a most *wicked law*, a crying shame to our land, a monstrous deformity in our social system, which must surely draw down upon us, as a people, the heaviest retributions of a righteous, a justly-offended, a long-suffering God. The proofs lie before us in this tract, with overwhelming force of demonstration, that this LAW corrupts the fountains of individual character, and poisons the stream of our national life; that it demoralizes our public men and sears the conscience of all concerned in administering it, hardening the heart of the educated judge, and rendering more brutal the lowest tipstaff on whom it devolves to enforce it; that it offers a bounty upon every act of inhuman daring, and drives the better-disposed to prevarication and stratagem to evade its cruel demands; altogether a curse and a disgrace to us as a nation, and deserving not to live another hour. Let every honest heart freely execrate it, and let it be consigned speedily to an infamous and eternal grave! In the words of DANIEL WEBSTER, uttered in his better days, concerning the Slave Trade, "It is not fit that the land should bear the shame longer." Let us at once and for ever disown it, as no law to us, and wash our hands of all complicity in this blasphemous defiance of Heaven, this heartless insult to whatever is honorable and good in man!

In this tract, no mention is made of that great company of slaves who, flying from their intolerable wrongs and burdens, are overtaken before reaching the Free States — (alas, that we should mock ourselves with this empty name of *free!*) —

and carried back into a more remote and hopeless slavery; nor of the thousands who, having fled in former years, and established themselves in industry and comfort in the Northern States, are compelled again to become fugitives, leaving their homes behind them, into a still more Northern land, where, under British law, they find at last a resting-place and protection; nor to any great extent of the numerous cases of white citizens, prosecuted, fined, harassed in every way, for the *crime* of giving shelter and succor to the hunted wanderers. To have included these — all emphatically *victims* of the Fugitive Slave Law — would swell our tract into a large volume. What a testimony against our land and our people is given by their accumulated weight! EVERY LIVING MAN AND WOMAN IS GUILTY OF THIS GREAT SIN, WHO EITHER BY APOLOGY OR BY SILENCE LENDS IT THE LEAST SUPPORT.

INDEX.

This Tract is for sale and to be obtained at the Anti-Slavery Offices, 5 Beekman Street, New York; 107 North Fifth Street, Philadelphia; 15 Steuben Street, Albany; and 221 Washington Street, Boston.   Price --- 12 cts. single; $10 per hundred.